THE ESSENTIAL
GREAT BIG
ASTON VILLA
QUIZ BOOK

CW01497094

A Comprehensive Compendium of
Challenges on Everything VILLA

Michael Baker

Unauthorised and Unofficial

1

Cover design by: Michael Baker

Table of Contents

Introduction

I remember standing on the Witton End terrace, midweek August 1974. as Villa celebrated something special (their Centenary) with a friendly against the then outstanding club in England: Leeds United.

It all seems to have moved quickly that we have now, celebrated a further half century of Aston Villa Football Club.

Of course that is the sort of trick that memory plays because once I started to go through old copies of the News and Record and YouTube clips it became crystal clear that a lot has happened in the continuing adventures of being a Villa Fan. Many memories of special times are still being forged. Indeed one of the best atmospheres I ever experienced was at the recent Champions League victory over Bayern Munich

Here in quiz format is a detailed journey through the history of Aston Villa. I have written the questions in the hope that they may evoke many memories, perhaps of events you witnessed in person as you tackle them. However you choose to use this book hope it brings you enjoyment.

Happy Quizzing and Reminiscing

Michael Baker, September 2025

About the Book

If you have bought one of my books before, you will be used to the fact that my question sets are of varying length. That is because I try to include questions that are worth asking rather than any padding and some seasons have been more eventful than others. Some of the questions between 1971-1983 have appeared in another book of mine: From Rotherham to Rotterdam, but there is still plenty of content that makes both books unique.

Question Set One – Champions League Season 2024/25

1. In August, who swapped their current squad number for the number 23?
2. Who was sent off after collecting two yellow cards in a pre-season defeat by RB Leipzig in New Jersey?
3. Who scored Villa's first Premier League goal of the 24/25 season?
4. Who started the away game at Leicester in the right back position after Matty Cash was injured early in the previous match against Arsenal?
5. Who scored two goals in Villa's thrilling 3-2 comeback at home to Everton?
6. Villa became the 11th English club to compete in the Champions League under its new name when they took the field against Young Boys and won 3-0. Which two Villa players had goals disallowed after VAR checks?
7. At which ground did Villa drop their first away points of the season?
8. Although their time in the Carabao Cup was short, Villa did negotiate an away tie against a club who were pushing Birmingham City hard in League One. Who did they beat 2-1?
9. Villa controversially set a ticket price of over £90 for their home Champions League matches. Who was the club's President of Business Operations, behind this decision?
10. And so on to Bayern Munich. Who had an opening goal for Villa ruled out by VAR in the First Half?
11. And who supplied the long pass from which Jhon Duran scored his wonder goal to win the game 1-0?
12. What Percentage possession did Villa have in that match? A: 30%, B: 35%, C: 40% or D: 45%
13. Villa ended a run by Bayern where they had gone unbeaten in how many consecutive CL group matches? A: 17, B: 29, C: 41, D: 53
14. Unsurprisingly, the next game with Manchester United was anti-climactic. It was the first home 0-0 draw at Villa Park for how many consecutive Premier League games? A: 32, B: 47, C: 62, D: 77
15. Villa won on the road after the next international break. coming from behind to win 3-1 at Craven Cottage. Who replied quickly for Villa to equalise Raúl Jiménez's 5th minute goal?

16. Who was adjudged by VAR to have handled the ball, conceding a penalty to Fulham that was subsequently saved by Emi Martinez?
17. Both teams ended the Fulham match with 10 men. Who was sent off for Villa?
18. Which Villa player was on the opposition bench when they beat Bologna in Match 3 of the Champions League Group stage?
19. Who opened the scoring against Bologna directly from a free-kick?
20. In the game at home to Bournemouth, which referee 'dished-out' 13 yellow cards?
21. Which goalkeeper was on the bench for Villa's home Carabao Cup defeat to Crystal Palace? A: Martinez, B: Olsen, C: Gauci or D: Zych
22. What nationality was the referee who awarded Club Brugge a controversial penalty kick in Villa's 1-0 Champions League defeat?
23. After that match, Villa then went on to lose a 4th game in a row. Where?
24. Who's penalty was saved by Dean Henderson in Villa's home 2-2 draw with Crystal Palace?
25. Who scored Villa's second in that match?
26. Villa's next opponents in the Champions League were Juventus. The match finished goalless thanks to a controversial VAR intervention right at the end to disallow who's effort?
27. Who scored their 10th goal in a Villa shirt as Villa ran out 3-1 winners at home to Brentford?
28. Back to winning ways in the Champion's League against a team from the former East Germany. In 1981/82 it was Dynamo Berlin. This time it was in Leipzig at which stadium?
29. Who gave Villa an early 3rd minute lead against RB Leipzig?
30. And what was the final score in this European match?
31. After a controversial loss away to Nottingham Forest, Villa welcomed Manchester City? Who's defence splitting pass put Morgan Rogers clear to set up Jhon Durán for Villa's opener?
32. Which referee sent Jhon Durán off in the Boxing Day match at St James' Park?
33. Newcastle assistant Jason Tindall came in for criticism from Villa. What seasonal, but very unfootball like t-shirt did he wear?

34. The New Year saw Villa back to winning ways against Leicester City. Who scored his first goal of the season to give Villa a 2-1 victory?
35. Which 18 year old made his first squad appearance for the first team with a place on the bench against Leicester City?
36. Celebrations at Villa Park for the nominated 150th anniversary match. An FA Cup tie versus West Ham. What colour was the special shirt worn by Villa to mark the occasion?
37. There was a one-off price for the News and Record for this game. In what season was it's regular price last £1.50?
38. Villa then played their last ever game at Goodison Park. Which two ex-Villains lined up for Everton?
39. Who's cross for Youri Tielemans' fantastic header marked the start of Villa's fightback at the Emirates?
40. Villa lost their next CL game in Monaco 1-0. In which part of the game did they concede the solitary goal? A: First ten minutes, B: Ten minutes before half time, C: Ten minutes into the second half or D: In added on time?
41. A quick return followed for West Ham, this time in the PL. Which player made their Villa debut from the bench?
42. Who was the main feature of the tifo displayed before the Celtic game?
43. Celtic became only the 4th Scottish team Villa had faced in a competitive match at CL week 8. Who were the other 3?
44. After an agonising wait, Villa learned they had qualified for the last 16 of the CL by finishing 8th in the table. How many of the teams finishing higher can you name?
45. Morgan Rogers became the 5th Villa player to score a hat-trick in European competitions. Can you name the other 4?
46. During a disappointing defeat to Wolves, Unai Emery made 4 half-time substitutions, can you name the players entering the field of play at this point?
47. Who did Villa knock out of the FA Cup at the 4th round stage?
48. Ipswich were the next PL visitors. Which one time Villa player was sent off in the 1-1 draw?
49. Next, Villa drew 2-2 with Liverpool. Who's backpass gifted Liverpool their opening goal?

50. Clearly unaware of the stunning pre-match shows at Villa Park, who reportedly surmised that Villa had a firework display perhaps because Liverpool were the visitors?
51. Who scored their first goals in a Villa shirt in the 2-1 win over Chelsea?
52. Two players made their 10th starting appearance for Villa in the FA Cup win over Cardiff. Who are they?
53. Leon Bailey put Villa ahead early against Club Brugge in their Round of 16 CL away tie, but who was credited with an assist?
54. What landmark number of starts for Villa did Jacob Ramsey reach in the away win at Brentford? A: 100, B: 150, C: 200 or D: 250
55. Robin Olsen kept a clean sheet against Brentford. This, at the time, reduced his average goals conceded per game for Villa to what? A: 1.5, B: 2.0, C: 2.5 or D: 3.0
56. Both John McGinn and Ollie Watkins made their 22nd appearance for Villa in European club matches. That is second only to which 2 club legends?
57. Marco Asensio became the 5th quickest ever Villa player to score a total of 7 goals, doing this over 8 games. Who tops the list with 7 in 3?
58. Which 3 Villa players appeared in Englands 2-0 World Cup Qualifier win over Albania?
59. Villa made it to the FA Youth Cup final with a 3-1 scoreline in the penalty shootout following a 1-1 draw with who?
60. How many league appearances did it take for Marcus Rashford to register his first Aston Villa PL goal?
61. Apart from Rashford, which other player scored their first PL goal for Villa in the 3-0 victory at Brighton and Hove Albion?
62. For what reason did Brighton have an equalising goal ruled out after a review by VAR? A: Foul (pushing), B: Handball, C: Offside D: Foul (tripping)
63. Unai Emery made 8 changes to the side that won at Brighton when the team started the next match with Nottingham Forest. How many of those eight players who started can you name?
64. A milestone was reached when Villa met Paris Saint-Germain in France. PSG became the latest, newest club that Villa have faced in League or Cup. How many opponent clubs had Villa met prior to them? A: 124, B: 149, C: 174 or D: 199

65. Who supplied the cross for Morgan Rogers to open the scoring in Paris?
66. Emery often names 2 substitute goalkeepers. Who was on the bench against PSG alongside Robin Olsen?
67. Still in Paris, who's early, harsh, yellow card potentially contributed to them being substituted at half time?
68. At Southampton, Marco Asensio missed two penalties, putting each in almost the same place. Was this to the goalkeeper's right or left?
69. How many substitutes scored in the 3-0 win over Southampton at St Mary's?
70. During the 2024/25 season, the News and Record for the First Team was sold at 4 different prices. What were they?
71. What words were on the pre-match tifo displayed before the home tie with PSG?
72. What was played mistakenly instead of the Champions League theme when the teams lined up?
73. Who provided the assist from which Ezri Konsa scored the match (sadly not the tie) winner to beat PSG 3-2?
74. Youri Tielemans was the last player to be substituted against PSG. Who replaced him?
75. Villa won a crucial match at home to Newcastle United next with Ollie Watkins scoring in the opening seconds and then being denied a perfect hat-trick by the woodwork. Did his left footed effort A: Score, B: Hit the Bar or C: Hit the post?
76. Who scored their first ever Premier League goal for Villa to put them 2-1 ahead against Newcastle?
77. Which substitute scored Villa's 4th to make the final scoreline: Villa 4 Newcastle 1?
78. Who was the only Villa player in the victorious Under-21 England Squad that won the Euro Trophy in Slovakia?
79. Who was fouled to earn Villa a penalty at Manchester City?
80. Which player made their 200th Premier League appearance when Villa played Fulham at home?
81. Ollie Watkins set a new all time scoring record for Villa in the Premier League with his winner against Bournemouth, what number of goals surpassed existing holder Gabby Agbonlahor's tally?

82. Who scored their first ever Premier League goal in the 2-0 home win against Tottenham Hotspur?
83. At the end of season awards, who won both the Supporters' Player of the Season and Players' Player of the Season?
84. John McGinn won the Goal of the Season Award for his strike against which club?
85. Villa's U-18 team won both the FA Youth Cup and their U-18 Premier League Final by beating the same opposition in both matches. Who did they defeat?
86. Who was the referee who wrongly disallowed Morgan Rogers' goal against Manchester United in the final game of the season?
87. Which player made the most starts for Villa in all competitions during the season?
88. Robin Olsen made a surprise appearance in his last game for Villa at Old Trafford following Emi Martinez's red card. Which club does he now play for?
89. Martinez's red card means he has been sent off twice while playing for Villa, but that is not the most as another current First Team player has seen the red card on 4 occasions. Who is that player?
90. In the close season 2025/26, full back Kosta Nedeljkovic agreed a second loan spell with which Bundesliga club?

5 Aside: The Current Squad

5 Aside: Emilio Martinez

1 While with Arsenal, Martinez was loaned out to six clubs, Getafe being one alongside five English clubs. How many of them can you name?
2 In which season did he win the FA Cup with Arsenal?
3 Martinez saved a penalty on his Villa debut. Who was the taker and who was he playing for?
4 How many clean sheets did Martinez keep in his first 100 Premier League games for Villa? A: 28, B: 31, C: 34 or D: 37
5 How many penalties did he save in the 2022 World Cup Final shootout?

5 Aside: John McGinn

1 Which club did John McGinn start his senior playing career at?
2 In a rare occurrence, John has played for Scotland in the same match with his brother. What is his first name?
3 McGinn scored Villa's first goal on their return to the Premiership. Who were the opponents?
4 In the same season, he suffered a fractured ankle in a match at Villa Park. Who were the visitors that day?
5 What has become his trademark goal celebration?

5 Aside: Evann Guessand

1 From which club did Evann join Villa?
2 Which country does he represent at International level?
3 What is Evann's shirt number for Villa?
4 His Villa debut came as a substitute, replacing which player who themselves had come on as a substitute?
5 Against which team did he make his first starting debut for Villa?

5 Aside: Jaden Sancho

1 True/False? Jaden has played in at least one Champions League Final
2 Has Jaden made more appearances for Manchester United or Chelsea?
3 His first two goals for England were scored in a home game against Kosovo where England won 5-3. Where was it played?
4 As of September 2025, how many England caps does he have? A: 12, B: 16, C: 19 or D: 23
5 Jaden took part in the penalty shootout in the 2020 UEFA Euro Final v Italy. Was his spot kick scored, saved or missed?

5 Aside: Harvey Elliott

1 In March 2025, Elliott scored the winning goal within a minute of coming on as substitute in a Champions League tie. Who were the opponents?
2 Which Championship club did he join on loan from Liverpool?
3 Elliott was named player of the tournament in England's victorious U-21 Euro Championship campaign of 2025. Who did he score against in the final?
4 Which club did he make his first ever senior appearance for?
5 His first Liverpool Premier League goal came in a rout of Bournemouth in 2022. What was the final score?

5 Aside: Matty Cash

1 Which club did Cash leave to play for Villa?
2 In the 2023/24 season, Cash opened his scoring account with two goals in the same game. Who were the opponents?
3 Which country does he represent at International level?
4 At the beginning of his senior career, Cash had a loan spell with a then, League Two club. Who were they?
5 At club level, Cash has, to date, scored two goals in European ties. Who has he scored against?

5 Aside: Tyrone Mings

1 What squad number did Mings wear during Villa's Championship promotion season?
2 Villa signed Mings from Bournemouth, but which club did he join Bournemouth from?
3 Mings made his debut for Villa away to which side?
4 Who did Mings score his first senior England goal against?
5 To date, Tyrone Mings has never been given a straight red card in his Villa career but he has been sent off twice. Can you name either of the opponents when this has happened?

5 Aside: Donyell Malen

1 For which country does Donyell play international football?
2 Which Premier League club did he join as part of his youth career?
3 Against which opponents did he score his first HOME Villa goal?
4 What is his squad number at Villa?
5 Which club did he make the greater number of appearances for: PSV or Borussia Dortmund?

5 Aside: Ezri Konsa

1 Ezri signed for Villa from Brentford, but which London club did he play for previously?
2 Konsa scored his first Villa goal in a cup tie, against which team?
3 In the 2023/24 season, he was called up for the first time to the England Senior squad for their matches against Malta and which other nation?
4 In 2020, Ezri was unfortunate not to be credited with a last gasp winner as his shot deflected in off Tyrone Mings to give Villa a much needed 2-1 home victory. Who did they beat?
5 Ezri made a substitute appearance in England's Last 16 match against Slovakia and started in the Euro 2024 Quarter-Final versus Switzerland. What number did he wear?

5 Aside: Youri Tielemans

1 Youri plays international football for Belgium. Which Belgian club did he begin his career with?
2 Which team did he score his first Premier League goal for Villa against?
3 Tielemans scored the only goal of the game to give Leicester City their first ever FA Cup Final win. Who did he score against?
4 Youri was a part of Belgium's Euro24 squad. Who did he score against after just 2 minutes in a group game?
5 Tielemans made his Villa debut away to Newcastle from the bench. Which player did he replace?

5 Aside: Ollie Watkins

1 Towards the beginning of his career, Watkins had a spell on loan with Weston-Super-Mare. Who were his parent club?
2 Which team did he score a hat-trick against in a Premier League home win in September 2023?

3 Although the club are currently with Adidas, Ollie can be seen advertising another sports brand in stores such as Sports Direct. Which manufacturer is it?

4 Ollie put England through to the Finals of Euro 2024 with a late goal against which opponents?

5 In February 2023 he set an all time Villa Premier League scoring record for scoring in consecutive matches. How many matches?

5 Aside: Lucas Digne

1 Lucas joined Villa after reportedly falling out with which manager?

2 Which club did Lucas score his first Villa goal against after Unai Emery became manager?

3 Lucas has had a rather distinguished playing career. Apart from Lille, which French club did he play for, and which Spanish club did he join later?

4 Lucas was voted Everton's player of the season in 2018/19, but it was shared with an ex Villa player. Who was he?

5 Digne was part of the France squad for which World Cup Finals tournament?

5 Aside: Pau Torres

1 Torres' first two goals for Villa were both scored away and were both equalisers. His first was against Wolves but who did he score the second against?

2 What squad number does Pau Torres have at Villa?

3 Which Spanish club did he join Villa from?

4 Pau scored his penalty in the 2021 Europa League Final shootout to help his side win 11-10. Who were the losing team?

5 What type of medal did he win at the 2020 Olympic Games?

17

5 Aside: Ian Maatsen

1 Ian was a member of which national squad at Euro 2024

2 While registered as a Chelsea player, Ian had loan spells with three EFL clubs. Two begin with the same letter. Can you name either?

3 Ian played in the Champions League Final 2024. For which team?

4 Which club did he score his first Champions League goal against. It came in the Quarter-Final stage

5 Which club did he help gain promotion to the English Premier League?

5 Aside: Ross Barkley

1 Ross started his senior career with Everton. During this period, he went on loan to two Yorkshire clubs. Can you name either?

2 True/False. Ross has made over 30 appearances for England?

3 With which team has he won the FA Cup with?

4 After his previous spell at Villa, Ross signed for which French club?

5 How many league goals did he score for Luton Town in the 2023/24 season?

5 Aside: Marco Bizot

1 Which club did Marco appear for in Champions League matches last season (24/25)

2 He has a full international cap for which country?

3 Who did he make his Premier League debut against?

4 During his career, the most club appearance have been for a team in the Eredivisie. Which one?

5 How tall is he?

5 Aside: Victor Lindelof

1 As of September 2025, Victor has 71 caps for which international side?
2 Which World Cup Finals Tournament has he played in?
3 Which manager signed him for Manchester United
4 Which European club did he leave to join Manchester United
5 True/False. Villa paid £8 million for him?

5 Aside: Emi Buendia

1 From which club did he sign for Villa?
2 Which club did he have a loan spell with during the 24/25 season?
3 True/False Emi has just one international senior cap for Argentina?
4 Against which team did he score his first Villa goal?
5 Which manager signed Emi for Villa

5 Aside: Boubacar Kamara

1 Who did Boubacar score his first, and so far only, senior Villa goal against?
2 In the 2023/04 season, against which team did he receive a red card?
3 Which club did he leave to sign for Villa?
4 Boubacar has played international football for France, but up until that point he was also eligible to play for which country?
5 What is his squad number at Villa?

5 Aside: Morgan Rogers

1 Which club did Morgan Rogers leave to sign for Villa?
2 Morgan scored his first goal for Villa against which team?
3 In the 2023/24 season, what shirt number did he wear for Villa?
4 Morgan had previously been on loan at two clubs with seaside connections. Can you name either?

5 Morgan's first senior league goals came in another loan spell at a then League One side. Who are they?

5-Aside: Unai Emery

1 Which month in 2022 was Unai Emery appointed to the head coach job at Villa Park?

2 As a player, from which clubs youth system did he graduate?

3 Which club did he manage between 2006-2008, taking them to promotion to La Liga for the first time in their history?

4 Who did Emery succeed as manager at Arsenal?

5 Which club did he manage to 3 Europa League titles?

Map Quiz 1: African Villans

Can you match the players to the location of the nation they can represent at international level?

Jonathan Kodjia, Mbwana Samatta, Curtis Davies, Bernard Traore, Marvelous Nakamba, Rudy Gestede, Albert Adomah, Habib Beye, Yannick Bolasie, Eric Djemba-Djemba, Yacouba Sylla, Moustapha Salifou, Trezeguet, Hassan Kachloul, Christopher Samba

Villanagrams 1

Can you rearrange the letters to reveal the names with Aston Villa Connections?

1 SNEAK WIN

2 MODERN MINISTER

3 TEETH WIPER

4 LIKING PENS

5 SAINTLIKE OWL

6 TRAP EUROS

7 REGAL HIJACKS

8 NAUGHTY TWIG HIM

9 NAE STAMINA

10 MEASLY CONTROL

11 RERUN TALISMAN

12 MR MOODY TETCHY

13 POLISH WOMAN

14 I TACKLE HERNIA

15 WINNERS ALE IDOL

16 UN GOAL SHY YE

17 TYING MERSON

18 SUDDEN ARENAS

19 HIM JOG MANY

20 BEATEN INCH STRIKE

Starting XI – Quiz 1

Can you name the players who kicked off the match in which Villa beat Bayern Munich 1-0 on 2nd October 2024?

Tenable – Quiz 1

Can you name the top 10 highest attended matches at Villa Park during the 2024/25 season? You might be surprised at some of the answers!

Number	Opposition
1st	
2nd	
3rd	
4th	
5th	
6th	
7th	
8th	
9th	
10th	

Question Set Two – A Rich History

SEASON 2024/25 *saw Aston Villa's 150th Celebrations so see how well you can answer these question sets on Villa's earlier times.*

Beginnings I - The 19th Century

1 Which competition began first, The Football League or The FA Cup?

2 William Scattergood was the first to do what for Aston Villa in their first ever game? A: Play as goalkeeper, B: Take a penalty kick C: Score a goal, D: Referee the match

3 Which pub on a junction with Wellington Road and Aston Lane became the headquarters of Aston Villa in the mid-1870's?

4 Villa's first ever Football League match was a draw with Wolverhampton Wanderers. Their first league win came in the next game against which club?

5 What position did Villa finish in the first ever Football League season?

6 Villa's highest ever win in a top division came in the 1891/92 season. Who did they beat 12-2?

7 In heraldry, what term is used to describe the position of the lion on the club badge?

8 The origins of Villa's badge are linked to Glasgow Rangers. Who introduced the Lion and 'Prepared' motto?

9 What synonym is used for the motto on Glasgow Rangers' badge?

10 The FA Cup was stolen from display in a local shop, 'Shillcocks' - a boot and shoe manufacturer - in 1895. On which road in Birmingham was the business situated?

11 What nationality was the first 'overseas' team to play a football match against Villa?

12 In what year was the first issue of the News and Record published? A: 1895, B: 1899, C: 1906, D: 1909

13 In 1895, Villa broke the then transfer record by paying Burnley how much to sign Billy Crabtree? A: £250, B: £500, C: £750, D: £1,000

14 On the way to their first FA Cup Final victory in 1887, Villa beat which team in the semi-final?

15 And, where was the semi-final played?

16 Villa beat West Bromwich Albion 2-0 in the 1897 FA Cup Final. Where was the match played?

17 What local sports paper first appeared in 1897?

18 In which year did Villa win the League and FA Cup double?

19 In April 1897, how did Villa player John Campbell make his mark on Aston Villa history forever?

20 Aside from his many football responsibilities, William McGregor had a Drapers store in which local thoroughfare?

Beginnings II - A New Century

1 Why did Villa postpone their 1st round FA Cup tie at home to Millwall in 1901?

2 Which prolific Villa forward scored both the goals to defeat Newcastle United in the 1905 FA Cup Final?

3 In 1913, a drinking fountain was set in the wall of which local bank in Lozells as a memorial to William McGregor?

4 What significant feature was removed from Villa Park in 1914?

5 True/False The 1914/15 season in Division One was completed in spite of World War 1 having already begun?

6 What FA Cup feat sets Howard Spencer aside from any other Aston Villa player?

7 Villa beat Chelsea in a 1920 FA Cup Semi Final. Why was this fortuitous for the FA?

8 Sam Hardy became a Villa goalkeeping legend. From which club did he sign for Villa?

9 Leeds City, left the Football League in 1919. Which player did Villa sign from them who went on to score in the 1920 FA Cup Final?

10 In 1920, Frank Barson and Clem Stephenson were transferred from Villa owing to a new policy. What was it?

11 Which Villa favourite scored a hat-trick of penalty kicks in a match with Bradford City in November 1921?

12 St John's churchyard in Perry Barr has a football shaped memorial to which Villa player who was shot and killed in 1924?

13 The White Horse Final was the first FA Cup final at Wembley stadium in 1923. What was the implication of the massive crowd for Villa supporters when they were finalists the following year?

14 When Villa played Arsenal at home in a tie in 1926, Villa Park saw an attendance above what figure for the first time? A: 50,000 B: 60,000 C: 70,000 D: 80,000

15 Which prolific scorer for Villa in a long career before the First World War, played for England and returned to Villa in 1927 for a short spell as reserve team coach?

16 In March 1928, over 23,000 turned up to witness 'Pongo' Waring make his debut in a Villa shirt. Why was this unusual?

17 Villa broke their goal scoring records in the 1930/31 season. Of the 42 league matches, in how many did Villa score at least 4?

18 'Pongo' Waring scored 4 goals on 3 separate occasions in 1930/31. How many league goals did he score in total that season?

19 Another Villa player scored 30 goals in the same season. Who was he?

20 In the 1930's, Villa often prepared for FA cup ties by visiting which Welsh coastal town?

21 Dai Astley was Villa's leading goalscorer in three consecutive seasons during the mid-1930's. Which country did he represent as an international?

22 In what year were Villa relegated from the top tier for the first time?

23 In that relegation season, Villa conceded 7 goals at home to three clubs. Can you name any one of them?

24 Blackburn Rovers were also relegated that year. In terms of historical reference, what was the significance of this happening to both clubs?

25 Although they were relegated, Villa scored quite a number of goals that season. Was it? A: 51, B: 61, C: 71, D: 81

26 Who took over as manager for Villa's first season in Division Two?

27 Villa's first game in Division Two was an away game where the Welsh National Anthem was sung before kick-off. Were the opponents? A: Cardiff City, B: Newport County, C: Swansea Town or D: Wrexham

28 In the season they were promoted back to Division One, Villa enjoyed a great FA Cup run. Who beat them in the Semi-Final?

29 Who was Villa's top goalscorer in the last full season before World War 2

30 The 1939/40 season was suspended after the first three games of the season. What was significant about Villa's kit in the opening match at home to Middlesborough?

Post-WWII Forties And Fifties

1 In 1946, Villa lost an FA Cup match 2-1 at Coventry. However they progressed to the next round. How was this possible?

2 How many goals did Trevor Ford score for Villa in their 1947 Boxing Day match against Wolverhampton Wanderers?

3 Peter Aldis scored just one goal for Villa. That was in 1952, but what was unusually special about it? A: It was direct from the kick-off, B: It went in after hitting a dog that ran on the pitch, C: It was the first ever scored from a bicycle kick outside the penalty area, D: It was a 35 yard header

4 From which local club did Villa sign centre-forward Bill Myerscough in 1955?

5 Villa's longest sequence of FA Cup replays came against Doncaster Rovers in 1955. Including the first tie as well as the replays, how many games were needed?

6 Who scored both Villa goals in their FA Cup Final victory over Manchester United in 1957

7 Which player from the 1957 cup final team owned a hardware shop in Wylde Green after retiring from football?

8 Which Villa forward was transferred on Boxing Day 1957 to Sheffield United where he became a goal-scoring club legend?

9 Which Villa forward scored on five occasions at the 1958 World Cup Finals?

10 For what reason did Villa play a home friendly against GAIS Gothenburg in October 1958?

11 Who replaced Eric Houghton as manager over the Christmas period of 1958?

12 Which one time Villa player became the first to score a total of 20 international goals for Wales?

13 From which club did player and future assistant manager Ron Wylie sign for Villa in 1958?

29

14 In the 1959/60 Division Two Championship season, no less than three Villa forwards scored at least 20 goals. Two were Hitchens and McParland, who was the third?

15 And who was the only ever present in that League campaign?

16 In their promotion season of 1959/60, Villa beat which London side 11-1 at Villa Park?

17 How many goals were scored by Gerry Hitchens in that 11-1 victory?

18 The weekend after the 11-1 win, Gerry Hitchens scored a hat-trick for Villa away to which club? (It was the same club that Villa beat at home to guarantee promotion).

19 Villa were knocked out of the FA Cup by Wolves in the 1959/60 season. At what stage?

20 Which player, who went on to score 70 goals was signed from Wolves in time to begin the 1959/60 season?

Villanagrams 2

Can you rearrange the letters to reveal more names with Aston Villa connections?

1 SHOOTS WEEDY LAW

2 MR SHOOTS WIDE

3 MRS GO ORANGER

4 MATCHES VENOM

5 NOT DRAWING WETS

6 KOALAS HAS LUNCH

7 GREATEST GOAT HUH

8 GREENGAGE BOOT

9 MAN TO CHAMP

10 MANURE SLOP

11 UNBALANCED OAR

12 TOUCHING HERO

13 VIVA COOL SEMIS

14 GOAL HANGER LOBBER I

15 TIGER SCOURGE

16 MEANLY RAKED

17 PENALTY VISITOR

18 AHA MR TRY GOAL

19 HIRE NEEDLE

20 GOAL SHY RENT

Starting XI – Quiz 2

Can you name the players who kicked off the match in which Villa came back from 0-2 to beat Coventry City 3-2 on 5th May 2001?

Tenable – Quiz2

Can you name the last ten different opponents that Villa have faced, to begin their programme of home games at the start of a new season. It does not matter if the first match was away, just who have they played first at home?

Number	Opposition
1st	
2nd	
3rd	
4th	
5th	
6th	
7th	
8th	
9th	
10th	

Question Set Three – The Fortune Swinging Sixties

The Warm-Up

1 In what year was the Holte End covered?

2 Who was Villa's top goal scorer from 1963/64 to 1965/66?

3 What was special about the 'characters' on the clock face situated on the old Witton Lane stand?

4 Tommy Cummings took over as Villa manager in 1967. He then went to his previous club and bought Dick Edwards and Tommy Mitchinson. Which club was this?

5 Before coming to Villa in the 1970's, which player was the first ever to take the field as a substitute and then score a hat-trick?

6 During the 1969/70 relegation season, Villa won only one game away from home. Who did they defeat?

7 Which player won the Terrace Trophy in consecutive seasons in 1967 and 1968?

8 Who succeeded Tommy Cummings as Villa Manager?

9 After failing to make the first team,, former Villa player David Evans went on to become an MP. He also banned away fans from which club in the 1980's?

10 Which of these did not play a World Cup match at Villa Park in 1966? A: Portugal, B: West Germany C: Argentina, D: Spain

Before the 1966 World Cup

1 The 1960/61 season saw the introduction of the Football League Cup. Who were Villa's first ever opponents in this competition?

2 Villa's biggest home win of the 1960/61 season was against Birmingham City. What was the score?

3 In the same season, Villa also suffered a 6-2 reversal against the club who also knocked them out of the FA Cup. Which team beat Villa?

4 Villa could not contest the League Cup Final in time for the end of the season, as in May, they went on a tour of which country?

5 Johnny Dixon retired after the final game of the 1960/61 season, a 4-2 win over Sheffield Wednesday, but which other legendary player made his Villa debut in the same match?

6 The delayed League Cup Final was played at the start of the 1961/62 season. Who did Villa beat over 2 legs?

7 Which newly signed forward got off to a good start, netting 3 goals in 4 games before being injured in a car crash that kept him out until December where he scored on his return?

8 Villa had two high scoring victories towards the end of the 1961/62 season. Firstly, they won 5-4 in London against which club?

9 They then also beat Leicester in a game that saw 11 goals. Was the score A: 6-5, B: 7-4, C: 8-3 or D: 9-2?

10 In the 1962/63 season Villa beat West Brom at the start of October. Who secured Villa's 2-0 win with a penalty, only to be sent off for fighting?

11 Phil Woosnam joined Villa. Where was he transferred from and who did he play international football for?

12 Why was Villa's pre Christmas home game with Manchester City abandoned?

13 Villa drew their FA Cup 3rd round tie at Bristol City on January 16th.1963. When did the replay take place? A: January 17th, B: January 23rd, C: February 13th, D: March 7th

14 Villa went on a terrible run of league defeats in the second half of the season. How many consecutive games did they lose between 23rd March and 4th May?

15 Villa finished runners up in the League Cup to Birmingham City. What was the score in the second leg at Villa Park?

16 In the 1963/64 season, Villa flirted dangerously with relegation. They did however thump Manchester United 4-0 at home. Which Manchester United legend was sent off in that game?

17 Which 4th Division team knocked Villa out of the FA Cup in 1963/64 season?

18 At the end of March, Villa played the same opponent on two consecutive days, first away, then at home. Who did they play against?

19 In 1964, the last FA Cup winning player from the 1957 team left Villa to play for Nuneaton Borough. Who was he?

20 George Graham left at the end of the season. Which London club did he join?

21 In the 1964/65 season, Villa had two ever presents. One was Charlie Aitken, who was the other?

22 Villa had to wait eight games for their first league win in the 1964/65 season. Who did they beat?

23 Villa reached the semi-finals of the League Cup. Who knocked them out?

24 Which goalkeeper joined in November 1964?

25 Harry Burrows left Villa in 1965, which Midlands rivals did he join?

26 The 1965/66 season saw Villa record two defeats against the only current league club that can boast a 100% **league** record over the Villa. Which team is this (they won both matches 2-1)?

27 In September, Graham Parker made his name in Villa history forever. What did he do?

28 Villa's Boxing Day match was abandoned. Who were the visitors to Villa Park?

29 In March, Villa left the field at half time at White Hart Lane, losing 4-1. What was the final score?

30 Two days later, Villa entertained a Dutch side, winning 2-1. Which club did they play?

After England's 1966 World Cup Victory

1 In September, 1966, Villa lost 5-0 at Leicester. Which ex-player returned to haunt them by scoring a hat-trick?

2 Villa's leading scorer in the 1966/67 season was also the first to score that season in the opening game at home to Newcastle United. Who was he?

3 After hosting 3 World Cup matches, Villa Park hosted a quarter-final in the FA Amateur Cup. What was the attendance? A: 8,410, B: 14,935, C: 24,920, D: 31,570

4 Which outfield player was ever present in the league, although he did miss the FA Cup tie with Preston North End?

5 Dick Taylor was sacked following the confirmation of relegation after the last home game of the season ended in a 2-4 defeat. Who beat Villa?

6 In the close season, the player who had arrived at Villa in 1959 with Charlie Aitken joined Falkirk on a free transfer. What was his name?

7 In 1967/68, Villa achieved the double over 3 teams as they got used to life in Division Two. Can you name any of them?

8 Who was Villa's top scorer in League and Cup that season?

9 In September 1968, Villa lost to Charlton Athletic at the Valley. Which future Villa player scored for The Valiants?

10 Villa's last home game was against a club that were promoted to Division One. Who were they?

11 In the 1968/69 season, the same club knocked Villa out of both the League and FA Cups. Which team?

12 The Villa News and Record of the 21st December carried a message from the new chairman, Doug Ellis. Who had he replaced?

13 The 21st December also heralded Tommy Docherty's first game in charge. Who were the visitors to Villa Park?

14 Which new signing scored on his debut, on Boxing Day, at home to Cardiff City?

15 Who became Villa's youngest ever player in September 1969 at the age of 15 years and 349 days?

Can you name the players who kicked off the match in which Villa beat Liverpool 7-2 on 4th October 2020?

Tenable – Quiz 3

Can you name the last 10 different kit suppliers Villa have had?

Number	Kit Suppliers
1st	
2nd	
3rd	
4th	
5th	
6th	
7th	
8th	
9th	
10th	

Question Set Four – From Rotherham to Rotterdam

Before we get into the memorable details of our seasons in Division 3, why not try these 10 straightforward teasers to get in the mood?

The Warm-Up

1 Who managed Villa to the third division title and promotion back to Division 2?

2 Against a backdrop of industrial unrest and power cuts, Villa bought in their own generator to ensure nothing would stop the appearance of Pele in a 1972 friendly with his Brazilian club team. Who did he play for?

3 Which Villa goalkeeper made his debut in the 71/72 6-0 away win to Oldham

4 The 1972 home match v Bournemouth was at that time the highest ever attended in the 3rd Division. How many spectators were present A: 37,213 B: 41,058, C: 45,842 or D: 48,110?

5 Who was Villa's regular penalty taker in their 3rd Division Championship winning season?

6 Which ex player who appeared nearly 200 times for Villa from 1958-65 was a very important coach and assistant to the manager?

7 It took Villa two seasons to be promoted from the 3rd Division. In their first attempt in 1970-71 they finished 4th. Which other team was promoted with Fulham?

8 Villa's training ground was officially opened in 1971. What is it called?

9 Although Villa had promotion rivals in Bournemouth and Notts County throughout the 1971-72 season, neither were promoted. Which team went up in second place?

10 Who did Villa meet in the 1971 League Cup Final at Wembley?

1970-71 A First Time for Everything

1 Villa began a whole new experience - 3rd Division Football - on Saturday 15th August 1970. What was unusual about the scheduled kick off time?

2 What colour was the top that Andy Lochhead usually wore during warm ups?

3 Villa beat 1st Division Burnley 2-0 in the second round of the League Cup. Who came on as a substitute and scored a great chipped goal for Villa's second?

4 Harry Gregory made his Villa debut in October 1970. Where was he signed from?

5 In the last match of October, Villa helped themselves to 5 goals in a 5-3 away win. Who did they beat?

6 In two of the most memorable matches for those who witnessed them, Villa beat a Manchester United containing Best, Charlton and Kidd to reach the League Cup Final. Andy Lochhead scored in both ties, but who headed Villa's winner in the second leg?

7 How many days before Christmas Day was the second semi-final against Manchester United?

8 In January, Villa's regular goalkeeper, John Dunn was involved in a car accident and missed a couple of games. Which player, still a teenager took over in goal?.

9 In the 1971 League Cup Final, which player cleared an Andy Lochhead effort off the line?

10 Who's two goals late in the League Cup Final put Villa on the wrong end of a 2-0 scoreline?

41

1971-72 The Long Road Back

1 Before the 71/72 season got underway, Villa played Birmingham City in a friendly that saw nearly 37,000 attend Villa Park. What was the score?

2 Villa started the 1971-72 season under torrential rain at home to Plymouth Argyle with a 3-1 win. This was marred to some extent by a bad ankle injury to which hero of the previous years League Cup run?

3 Villa began their League Cup campaign with a protracted series of encounters with Wrexham. At which neutral venue did Villa finally win their 2nd replay?

4 Ray Graydon scored his first Villa goal in a 2-0 home win over Rochdale. From which club was he signed?

5 At the end of September, Villa suffered their first home league defeat of the season to a team who were bottom of the table at the time. Who won 1-0

6 In November, Villa played Port Vale at Vale Park with the match ending in a rather unusual scoreline. What was the result?

7 For the second season running, in spite of their proud record in the FA Cup, Villa went out again in the first round. Both opponents are not currently in the top 4 divisions of English football. Who were they?

8 Still in November, Villa beat promotion rivals Notts County at Villa Park 1-0. Which Villa goalkeeper saved a penalty taken by Don Masson?

9 After some poor results, a change of fortune began before November arrived as Villa ran riot against Blackburn Rovers scoring four goals at the Witton End to end the first half 4-1. What was the full time score?

10 And better still to come in November when Villa won 6-0 away to Oldham Athletic. Who scored a hat-trick?

11 A week before Christmas, Villa beat Bolton Wanderers 3-2. Among the scorers was an unlikely candidate who went on to score 3 more before the end of the season. Who was the player?

12 On January 1st, Villa beat Halifax Town by a single Ray Graydon goal. How did the cover of the Villa News and Record herald the New Year?

13 In a mid-January midweek match at Villa Park, Villa beat Shrewsbury Town 3-0. Which player made a rare assist for the third goal which was scored by Andy Lochhead?

14 On 12th February, Villa came from behind to beat close rivals Bournemouth 2-1. This unforgettable match was featured on Match of the Day. What colour shirts did Bournemouth wear?

15 Chris Nicholl made his debut in March after signing from which club?

16 Unlike today's fixture schedule, Villa played three games in four days over the Easter break. They won all three. Can you name any of the teams they beat?

17 Still in early April. Who scored Villa's 90th minute goal to gain two points at home to Oldham as Villa won 1-0 to make it five wins in ten days?

18 Villa clinched promotion with a 1-1 draw at Mansfield. Which Centre Back came in for Chris Nicholl to play his final match not only for Villa but also of a very successful career which had made him a legend at Coventry City?

19 Villa clinched the title with a 5-1 thrashing of Torquay United at home. Which legendary Villa player made his full first team debut and also scored?

20 Villa finished with their 32nd win of the season at home to the same club as the one they met on their first ever game as a 3rd division side. Who were the opponents?

21 At the time, in winning the title, Villa recorded the highest points total ever for the 3rd division champions. How many points did they amass?

22 Who won the Terrace Trophy for the 71/72 season? A: Bruce Rioch B: Ray Graydon C: Andy Lochhead or D: Jimmy Cumbes

23 Just one team held Villa to a draw at Villa Park during the 1971/72 season who were they?

24 Villa also enjoyed success in the FA Youth Cup beating which team 5-2 on aggregate in the Final?

25 Villa only lost eight times in the league during the 1971-72 season and were also the only team to have a healthy goal average over 2, How many

points did they take on their South Coast travels at Plymouth, Torquay, Bournemouth and Brighton?

1972-73 Upward Momentum

1 Villa ended their pre-season in an unexpected way by playing in the FA Charity Shield at home to Manchester City where they lost to the only goal of the game – a penalty kick scored by which England international?

2 While Leeds United sported their numbers on sock tags, Manchester City players also had their numbers in an unconventional place. Where on their kit was this?

3 Villa opened their home Division Two campaign with a 2-1 victory against a club newly relegated from the First Division. Who were they?

4 In the first round of the League Cup, Villa won 4-1 against a team who earlier in the year had entered FA Cup folklore forever with one of the greatest ever giant killings. Which team did they beat?

5 Towards the end of August, which player aged 18, made his Villa debut against Carlisle United? He went on to make 196 starting appearances and become a firm favourite at the club.

6 John Robson made his Villa debut at Sheffield Wednesday on 23rd December. From which club was he signed?

7 Early in the new year, Villa were thumped at home 3-0 by which promotion rival? Over their two league matches Villa scored 1 and conceded 7 to them. Who were they?

8 At the end of January, Willie Anderson played his last Villa match in a 3-2 defeat to Everton in the FA Cup. Who was he transferred to?

9 Which Villa player was sent off in a bad tempered match at Millwall toward the end of the season?

10 Villa's last game of the season saw them continue an unbeaten run of seven matches as they drew 2-2 with Carlisle United. Which regular defender from Villa's 3rd division days scored for Carlisle?

11 Andy Lochhead played his last Villa match against Carlisle United. Which team did he move to?

12 Villa finished the season in third place behind Burnley and QPR but were not promoted to the first division. For what reason?

1973-74   99 Not Out

1 Villa started the 1973/74 season against the same club they opened the previous season; Preston North End. Which football legend was their manager at the time?

2 Trevor Hockey scored on his Villa debut in the opening game of the 1973/74 season. Which club was he signed from?

3 Who scored a brilliant thirty-yard effort and then a thunderbolt free-kick in consecutive home matches against Fulham and Leyton Orient in September 1973?

4 Villa's first defeat of the season came right at the end of September with a 2-0 defeat at Notts County. Who was their well respected manager who later returned to manage them in two future spells after a stint at Sheffield United?

5 Boxing Day 1973 saw Villa play a local derby where they lost 2-0 to WBA. Both goals were scored by which player?

6 In the 4th round of the FA Cup Villa drew 1-1 away to Arsenal in spite of going down to ten men. Which player was sent off after a controversial incident with Bob Wilson?

7 Four days later a crowd of nearly 48,000 witnessed Villa beat Arsenal in the 4th round replay. Bob Wilson playing pantomime villain could not keep Villa out as they won by what score?

8 In February, Bruce Rioch was transferred to which First Division club?

9 In March, Villa thrashed Portsmouth 4-1 with a second half goal blitz. Which striker made his home Villa debut in this game?

10 Villa lost both league games against Blackpool. What was unusual about the scheduling of their matches home and away?

11 Bobby Campbell made his Villa debut from the bench in the 2-1 defeat to Sunderland in April. Which goalkeeper also made his debut?

12 Villa's last home match of the season was a friendly against a top Dutch side shortly before their National team won so many plaudits reaching the World Cup Final. Was it against A: Ajax, B: Feyenoord, C: PSV Eindhoven or D: Twente Enschede?

1974-75   A Very Special Centenary

1 Villa's Pre-Season included a friendly to mark Villa's Centenary celebrations against First Division Champions: Leeds United. Who was their manager?

2 The Centenary match programme contained an all time table of leading first division clubs since 1888. Villa were in second place with 2669 points. The team above them were also the team Villa had played the most. Which team?

3 For the 1974/75 season, Villa introduced a standing season ticket. What was the price to non-shareholders? A: £10 B: £15, C: £20 or D; £25

4 From which club did both manager Ron Saunders and midfielder Frank Carrodus join Villa?

5 The Ron Saunders campaign era began with a 1-1 draw away to a club who nowadays currently play their football in National League North. Who were these opponents?

6 By the time of just the 4th league match Villa had played Hull City twice. Villa trounced them in the home game, beating them by what scoreline to send out a message to the rest of the division?

7 Goalkeeper Graham Moseley joined Villa for a short loan spell playing 3 matches. Who were his parent club?

8 Villa's journey to the League Cup Final began with a thumping 3-0 replay win away to which First Division team?

9 In September, Leighton Phillips made his Villa debut from the subs bench in a 3-0 home win over Millwall. Which player scored a hat-trick in this win? A: Ray Graydon, B: Brian Little, C: Keith Leonard or D: Sammy Morgan

10 John Gidman was sent off at Oldham and returned for only one match after suspension before he suffered an eye injury. What was the cause? A: An opponents boot, B: A piece of swarf while doing DIY C: A scratch from a tree branch or D: A firework

47

11 Apart from the final against Norwich City, Villa played every team they met in their League Cup run twice, with one exception. Which team?

12 Which 4th Division team were beaten by Villa over 2 legs in the League Cup semi-final?

13 Bobby McDonald scored in the first leg of the semi-final but he was not Villa's youngest player on the field that night. Who was?

14 In the 4th round of the FA Cup, Villa Park witnessed a 4-1 thumping of which First Division side who had players such as Len Badger, Eddie Colquhoun and Bill Dearden in their team?

15 A photo in the February programme for the home match with Manchester United captured Ron Saunders with his Manager of the Month award. What was it?

16 Who scored his first goal of the season in the 2-0 home defeat of Manchester United?

17 When Villa advertised their 17 'Football Special' trains to get fans to and from Wembley, how much was the return fare? A: £1.15, B: £2.50, C: £4.00 or D: £5.75

18 Who's handball conceded the penalty awarded to Villa in the League Cup Final at Wembley?

19 Who was the ex Villa goalkeeper who saved Ray Graydon's penalty kick for Norwich City?

20 At Wembley, did Ray Graydon place his penalty kick to the goalkeeper's right or left?

21 Which future chairman of Villa had been newly appointed to the board of directors - his first game in that post being the League Cup final?

22 Villa paraded the League Cup at their next home game to Bolton Wanderers which typically ended in an anti-climatic goalless draw. Which future England manager was in Bolton's defence?

23 Villa Player's released a single in March 1975. What was it called?

24 .What unusual method was employed to dry the pitch so the home game with Southampton could go ahead?

25 In April, Villa thrashed Oldham 5-0 at Villa Park. A penalty that normally would have been taken by 'Chico' Hamilton was passed on to another player so he could get his hat-trick. He missed but scored a third later in the game. Who was the player?

26 Villa secured promotion with a big win away to Sheffield Wednesday who would be relegated at the end of the season. What was the score?

27 A crowd of over 57,000 witnessed Villa's 2-0 victory in the last home game of the season? Their opponents who provided a guard of honour to welcome the Villa players on to the pitch were still chasing promotion themselves. Who were they?

28 Villa's home record showed they lost one game during the season and conceded a total of how many goals? A: 6, B: 12 C: 18 or D: 24

29 Brian Little finished top goalscorer for league matches in the 2nd Division. However another Villa player scored even more when Cup matches were taken into account? Which player was this?

30 Villa played Stoke City at the end of the season in a testimonial match for which Villa player?

1975-76 Back in the Top Flight

1 Apart from the typeface, what major change was made to the appearance of the cover of the Villa News and Record in time for the 1975/76 season?

2 Who were Villa's opponents in their first Division One match in 1975?

3 Who scored Villa's first goal on their return to first division football in 1975?

4 In August 75, Norwich City got their own back for last years League Cup final defeat and end of season 4-1 thumping by beating Villa 5-3 at Carrow Road. Which striker, an adversary going back to the 3rd division games with Bournemouth scored a hat-trick for Norwich?

5 When Villa beat Manchester City 1-0 Which player lowered his shorts to his knees in response to being booed by the crowd as he prepared to take a corner at the Witton End?

6 In mid-September, which striker scored a late goal to cement Villa's 2-0 home win over Arsenal only for a career ending injury to follow, meaning this was his last ever competitive game?

7 Who were Villa's first ever opponents in European competition when they played in the 75/76 UEFA Cup tournament?

8 At the end of September, Villa came back from 1-0 down to beat Birmingham City. Which player made a bad tackle on John Robson sparking a melee and later lost the ball to Brian Little who gratefully drove home the winner delighting the majority of fans in the near 54,000 crowd?

9 Which Birmingham striker was substituted for Gary Pendry?

10 New signing Andy Gray was watching from the dugout at the Birmingham game. Which club had he signed for Villa from?

11 Which goalkeeper made his Villa debut in the win over Birmingham City?

12 Unable to turn things around at home, what was the aggregate score over the 2 legs of Villa's only tie of their UEFA Cup campaign?

13 After a November defeat at Ipswich, Villa enjoyed a return to form with a 5-1 home win against which team who were to finish rock bottom of the First Division?

14 On Boxing Day, Dennis Mortimer made his debut after signing from which club?

15 Who did Villa beat 4-1 on Boxing Day at Villa Park?

16 Villa made an early FA Cup exit in a 3rd round replay defeat to the club who went on to win the trophy that year. Which club?

17 Early in February a Villa side hit by injuries went down 2-1 to Manchester City at Maine Road. Defender John Overton was a newcomer to the first team while another debut from the subs bench gave which Villa legend his debut aged 17?

18 In March, Villa drew 2-2 with Leicester. Incredibly, the same player scored all 4 goals. Who?

19 How many matches did Villa win away from home in their first season back in Division One?

20 Villa finished with the 3rd highest average attendance that season. Which two clubs had more?

1976-77 Goals, Goals, Goals, Replays, Replays, Replays

1 Villa began the 76/77 season in style at Villa Park. The result a 4-0 drubbing of West Ham. Which future Villa goalkeeper was in the nets for The Hammers?

2 In September, Andy Gray scored a hat trick in the home game versus Ipswich Town. The last time a Villa player achieved this in the First Division was in the year England won the World Cup. Who was that forward?

3 Still in September, Birmingham City won their league match at Villa Park 2-1. Which Villa player ran the ball almost the full length of the pitch before delivering the cross from which Andy Gray scored Villa's goal?

4 International call ups meant the home game with Arsenal was postponed and instead the 9th October was given to an infamous home friendly against Glasgow Rangers. Due to crowd trouble it was abandoned. What was the scoreline at the time?

5 Which midfield player scored his first goal for Villa in their 1-0 victory at Sunderland shortly after his transfer from Arsenal?

6 Although going behind to an Alan Ball goal, Villa smashed Arsenal 5-1 at home. Which future Villa manager was in the opposition line-up, which also included Jimmy Rimmer in goal?

7 Charlie Young made his debut in the abandoned match with Glasgow Rangers and so his official league debut took place in December in a 3-1 victory over Leeds United at Elland Road. What position did he play?

8 In a very unique set of circumstances local business Fort Dunlop celebrated 60 years by collaborating with Villa to hold a friendly with which West German club?

9 December 15th 1976 saw a midweek match that will always be in the memory of Villa fans as they demolished Liverpool 5-1 at Villa Park. Who were the three Villa goalscorers?

10 And what was the half time score?

11 Into the New Year and after the first 2 matches vs QPR failed to produce a winner even after extra time in the League Cup Semi-Final, the tie went to a third match at which neutral venue?

12 Villa reached Wembley with a 3-0 win over QPR who was the hat-trick hero?

13 The League Cup Final against Everton at Wembley was an anti-climatic goalless draw. The 96,000 plus crowd were perplexed when referee Gordon Kew called the two captains together shortly after half time and the players then wandered round looking at the pitch for a bit. For what reason?

14 The League Cup Final replay ended 1-1 after extra time. At which clubs ground was this fixture played?

15 Before the next replay Villa were knocked out of the FA Cup at the quarter-final stage in spite going ahead really early through a 35 yard wonder goal by Brian Little. Who were their opponents?

16 Villa's equaliser came in the 80th minute with a thunderbolt from who?

17 With the match seeing one more goal scored apiece in quick succession it was left to Brian Little to score the winner late into extra-time. Who supplied the cross into the penalty area which took a slight but crucial deflection?

18 Which defenders mistake in leaving the ball let Little pounce for the winner?

19 True or False, the same referee took charge of all three Final matches?

20 Villa lost away 2-1 to Birmingham in May having to play about an hour with ten men after which player was sent off?

21 Which Birmingham player was also dismissed but much later in the match?

22 Unsurprisingly, Villa had significant fixture congestion as they headed towards the end of the season playing about a third of their entire league fixtures at an average of around every three days. In the last match of the campaign, they beat WBA by what scoreline?

23 What position did Villa finish in the First Division 1976/77?

24 Big favourite and captain Chris Nicholl left in the close season to join which club?

25 After some infrequent appearances a substitute, Keith Masefield made his only start for Villa in a match near the end of the season at Tottenham Hotspur. What position did he play?

1977-78 Return to European Action

1 Villa opened the season with a 2-1 win at QPR. 3 players made their debut: Jimmy Rimmer, Ken McNaught and which player who would become a future Villa manager?

2 Villa went into an early lead in their first home match but were then beaten 4-1 by Manchester City with two goals conceded late in the game. Who scored a hat-trick for the visitors?

3 The next home match was a defeat to Everton. This game marked what significant change to Villa Park?

4 Villa began their UEFA Cup campaign with a 4-0 home victory against which Turkish club?

5 Villa lost their home match with Birmingham City to a solitary Keith Bertschin goal. But who was their manager?

6 In October, supporters felt a little unease when reports emerged that Ron Saunders had been offered a very lucrative opportunity to manage which national team?

7 Two goals from Ken McNaught gave Villa a home win on the next round of the UEFA Cup, this time against which opponents from Poland?

8 In November Villa put in a tremendous performance to win at Anfield. What was the score?

9 By the time of the next UEFA cup tie with Athletic Bilbao, radio listeners had become accustomed to the invitation to 'Get your Prayer Mats Out' by which local presenter?

10 This was accompanied by a suggestion listeners should 'Hail Saunders of the Villa' to which tune performed by Norman 'Hurricane' Smith under a different name? It became synonymous with Villa being played over the PA during the last 50 years and still going strong.

11 In January, Tommy Craig made his Villa debut after signing from which club?

12 Villa were drawn against Barcelona in the quarter-finals of the UEFA Cup with the first leg at Villa Park. After hours spent queuing for tickets, match day came around and Villa fans finally had their chance to see which legendary footballer who also scored Barcelona's opening goal?

13 David Evans was surprisingly given his debut in this vital match. What position did he play?

14 The match ended in exciting fashion as Villa clawed back a 2 goal deficit with goals in the last 5 minutes. Who were Villa's scorers?

15 The return leg in Spain saw Villa play for over an hour with 10 men after having which player sent off?

16 For those at home, radio listeners followed the match and although they were invited once more to 'get on your knees' and 'Hail Saunders' Villa were knocked out. What was the aggregate score?

17 In March, Villa had the opportunity to bring Nottingham Forest's unbeaten run to an end, but ultimately it was Forest who grabbed a late winner to win 1-0. Who scored?

18 Which team were beaten 2-0 at Villa Park on Easter Monday and were relegated?

19 Villa's last home game was against FA Cup finalists Ipswich Town. Ipswich clearly had their focus on the following week as Villa overwhelmed them to win by what score? A: 4-1 B: 5-1 C: 6-1 or D: 7-1

20 Two players were ever present for the 1977/78 season: Dennis Mortimer and who else?

1978-79 Million Pound Footballers

1 Pre-season in 1978 saw Villa play 3 matches in Yugoslavia. Their opponents were Rijeka, Olympia Ljubljana and which club from Split?

2 Villa started the new league season at home with a 1-0 win over Wolves. Which player, signed from Walsall in January made his full debut?

3 A current Villa team played against a Villa 74/75 team in a testimonial for Keith Leonard, but how did Villa also play against Villa in their first away match of the 78/79 season?

4 Villa lost the next match on their travels 1-0 to Bristol City. They also gave a player who was pivotal in their 80/81 First Division Championship season a debut from the bench. Which player made this debut?

5 In October, Villa drew 2-2 at home to Manchester United. Which 20 year old signed from Arthurlie, Glasgow who was only to make 3 first team appearances for Villa was given his full debut?

6 Villa needed two replays to get past Crystal Palace in Round 3 of the League Cup. What neutral venue hosted the decisive tie?

7 Villa beat Birmingham City 1-0 St Andrews thanks to a swift counter attack started by Jimmy Rimmer and finished by Andy Gray. This brought to an end a run of how many consecutive defeats at the hands of our near neighbours?

8 Middlesbrough were quickly proving themselves to be Villa's bogey team. Their 2-0 win at Villa Park in October did nothing to change this. What was the reason this match was rearranged to a Friday evening? A: There was a big protest planned against Government cuts on Saturday, B: Several players were called up for internationals later next week and needed time to rest, C: A rail strike was planned for the weekend, D: The Motor Show was on at the NEC.

9 On Boxing Day, a 2-2 home draw with Leeds United was also memorable for the way one fan tried to get a better view. What did they do?

10 The cover of the News and Record for the home match with Derby County in April was an action picture of Andy Gray. For what reason was that somewhat ironic?

11 On Easter Monday, Villa, once again beat Liverpool at home. Which defender was encouraged to play as a forward in the 3-1 win?

12 And strangely, which forward ended up playing in defence in the next match where Villa won 2-1 at Carrow Road?

13 Still in April, after falling behind to a very early goal by Frank Stapleton, Villa smashed Arsenal 5-1 at home. Who was the player who scored a hat-trick?

14 Villa then beat Chelsea 2-1. Which ex Villa player was their manager at the time?

15 In May, Villa were held 2–2 at home by Ipswich Town. Which Dutch player scored both their goals??

1979-80 Comings and Goings

1 Villa's final campaign of the 1970's began with a 1-1 draw at Bolton Wanderers. Tony Morley caught the eye of the press as he made his debut. Where did Ron Saunders sign him from?

2 The cover of the programme for Villa's first game of the season pictured Morley and which other player who had signed in the close season from Grimsby Town?

3 Villa needed a penalty shootout to resolve their first League Cup tie which ended in a nail-biting 9-8 victory. Which Third Division side did they beat when their goalkeeper missed his penalty?

4 Joe Ward made his last of his 3 Villa appearances against Crystal Palace. Unusually, his other two were made against which same high profile club over two different seasons?

5 Joe Ward's transfer to Hibernian was instrumental in the acquisition of which soon to become highly influential player who moved the other way?

6 And continuing that theme, John Gidman moved to Everton early into the season. Which player had moved the other way a few games earlier?

7 The start of November saw matters off the field proving a distraction. In a boardroom battle, Doug Ellis lost out with his efforts at an Extraordinary General Meeting to oust Ronald and Donald Bendall together with which Villa chairman?

8 The change of personnel at Villa continued with the playing staff, this time John Deehan was transferred to which rival club?

9 An incident packed home win over Stoke saw a late penalty and a sending off. But what unusual, although not unique occurrence, had the Holte End singing. 'Hello, Hello, Andy is back'

10 Which former Villa player and manager announced they would be leaving the board of directors at the end of the decade?

11 The last home game before Christmas saw Villa soundly beat Coventry City 3-0. In addition to Bobby McDonald, their team featured 3 more

players who also played for Villa either before or in the future. How many can you name?

12 Boxing Day 1979 saw Villa lose 2-1 at Nottingham Forest. Who was a surprise inclusion at goalkeeper with Jimmy Rimmer indisposed?

13 Villa's next match over the festive period was a 3-1 win at Ashton Gate. Who scored their first top division hat-trick?

14 In February 1980, Crystal Palace were the first of that month's visitors to Villa Park. Who was their manager?

15 Villa reached the quarter-finals of the FA Cup where they were knocked out by an injury time penalty at West Ham. Who scored this only goal of the game?

16 In March, Villa's injury list was so vast that they had to play defenders as strikers against Ipswich. Allan Evans wore the number 9 at Villa Park. Who wore the number 8 shirt?

17 Villa then beat another East Anglia side, Norwich 2-0. Still without strikers, Pat Heard made his debut. Another made his debut from the bench and scored. Who was this player that only made 2 more appearances for Villa before joining Birmingham where he played many times, scoring 29 goals?

18 In April, another youngster made his debut, again making only a few senior appearances in their Villa career, before going on to play nearly 100 times for Birmingham. Who was this?

19 Sadly, Brian Little played his last game toward the end of this season before being forced to retire through injury. How old was he when he stopped playing?

20 Villa won the FA Youth Cup for the first time since 1972. Who did they beat in the final?

1980-81 'Do You Want to Bet Against Us?'

1 In the 1980/81 season, Villa went out of both domestic cup competitions early in the tournaments. Who knocked them out of the League Cup?

2 Which team did Peter Withe make his Villa league debut against?

3 And at which ground did he score his first Villa goals?

4 Of course, Villa did not lose many league matches this season, but who were the first to beat Villa in the 80/81 First Division fixtures?

5 In September, Villa beat Wolves 2-1 at Villa Park. Which Wolves player scored an own goal?

6 Extended TV highlights of Villa's October home match with Sunderland showed Peter Withe having little luck in scoring his first home goal. Fortunately others were on target. What was the score in this comprehensive Villa win?

7 Both of Villa's matches against Manchester United ended in the same scoreline. What was it?

8 Villa's first home score draw was against Leeds United in November. Gary Shaw equalised after which Argentinian footballer had put the visitors ahead?

9 Villa met Birmingham City for the second time just before Christmas. In the BBC TV match commentary by Barry Davies it was noted that the youngest players on each side at kick off were Gary Shaw and Phil Hawker. What else did they have in common for this particular derby fixture?

10 In that match, Villa smashed Birmingham 3-0 with three second half goals. Who scored 2 of them?

11 .After losing top spot with a surprise defeat at Brighton, Villa returned to first position with a 1-0 Boxing Day win over which Midlands rivals?

12 .The Boxing Day match also witnessed a sad occasion when the recent passing of a Villa legend was marked. *Pongo* Waring scored a record 49 goals in one season for Villa in 1930-31 season. In total he scored 171 goals

while with the club. Although widely known by his nickname, what was his actual first name?

13 In January, Villa beat Liverpool 2-0 at home. Who scored the late goal that cemented this victory?

14 Two of the Liverpool team that day shared the same surname. Who are they?

15 The Liverpool game also witnessed what significant addition to the Villa Park stadium?

16 At Goodison Park, the opening goal in Villa's 3-1 victory over Everton was voted Goal of the Season on Match of the Day. Who scored it?

17 Who was Villa's regular penalty taker during this season?

18 While Bob Champion was winning the Grand National on Aldaniti, Villa impressively won away 4-2. Who were their opponents?

19 Which player's misplaced backpass allowed Peter Wither to grab a late winner v WBA much to the relief of the majority in Villa Park?

20 Ipswich Town returned to Villa Park after playing there in an FA Cup semi-final three days before. Who did they lose that match to?

21 A crowd of over 47,000 with some locked out and following the match by watching the scoreboard and listening from the park on Trinity Road witnessed the top of the table clash with Ipswich. Villa conceded an early goal aided by a mistake by which defender?

22 Villa went further behind to a goal by Eric Gates, again aided by a mistake by which midfielder?

23 Villa's got back into the game with a great strike by which player to make it 1-2? (A reward for all the training on shooting with his weaker foot).

24 Villa's last home match was against Middlesbrough. In a later interview discussing how they had become a bogey team, which player stated that he, at the time had never been on the losing side against them?

25 The Middlesbrough match saw Villa win comprehensively 3-0. There was a certain amount of premature title celebrating within the crowd owing

to misinformation about the score in the match between Ipswich and which opponents?

26 Which giant of world football made an appearance before the crucial end of season match at Highbury and got boos from the Villa end as he paraded an Arsenal scarf?

27 Which two players scored Arsenal's goals in their 2-0 win over Villa??

28 Although they lost their final match, Villa had already done the hard work to accrue enough points as their nearest rivals Ipswich lost both their remaining games. Confirmation came at full time as they went down 2-1 to Middlesbrough. Who scored both Middlesbrough goals?

29 .How many games did Arsenal lose at home in the 1980-81 season?

30 What was taking place at Wembley that contributed to serious traffic congestion and late in the day arrival for players and fans at Arsenal?

1981-82 Champions of Europe

1 Before starting their defence of the title, A pre-season friendly at Villa Park saw them beat which national team 4-2?

2 Villa's pre-season warm up also included an appearance against Spurs in the FA Charity Shield at Wembley. What was the final score?

3 The opening game of the 1981-82 season saw a crowd of nearly 32,000 welcome the defending champions and Ron Saunders onto the Villa Park pitch. Then in a typically anti-climactic fashion they lost 1-0 to which newly promoted side?

4 When Villa got their first win of the season on the road. Terry Donovan scored twice in a 3-1 victory. Over which club?

5 Which other English team competed in the 1981/82 European Cup tournament?

6 Villa's first European Cup tie was against FC Valur. Which country are they from?

7 The programme also had a big feature on all the European participants. One interesting tie in the list of first round matches in the European Cup was Vainqueur Tour v FC Zurich. Where were Vainqueur Tour from?

8 In October, Villa played Wolves three times. Which player scored for Wolves and was later sent off in the League Cup tie at Villa Park?

9 Around this time there was a significantly intensive advertising campaign by a brand named *Winners*. This included promotions in the matchday programs and an offer of money off the admission price to the home match with Arsenal. What were they marketing?

10 The next round of the European Cup was against Dynamo Berlin. Who scored Villa's winner in the away first leg with a solo run from well inside his own half?

11 After winning 3-0 in the league at Molineux, Villa returned a few days later in the League Cup return. Who scored both goals in Villa's 2-1 win?

12 What was the score in the home leg of the European Cup tie with Dynamo Berlin?

13 In December Villa lost 1-0 to Man City with a goal that would more than likely never be allowed nowadays. The reason being the referee allowed a quick free kick to be taken while which Villa player suffered a head wound that needed stitches?

14 The New Year began with Villa thumping a team 6-0 at their own ground in the FA Cup. Who scored a hat-trick and who were the opposition who ironically did the double over Villa in the league?

15 The quarter-final was the furthest Villa could progress in the League Cup, going down 1-0 with ten men at home to which rivals?

16 What was Ron Saunders last match as Villa manager?

17 Against the rumours that Ron Saunders may be taking over at Birmingham City, Villa's away support let their feelings know at St Andrews as Villa won 1-0 thanks to a goal by who?

18 Dynamo Kiev were the next opponents in the European Cup. Where was the away leg played due to winter weather conditions?

19 Who was the star Dynamo Kiev player in their team who is still their record goalscorer and who played in two World Cups?

20 What was the score in the away leg of the European Cup tie with Dynamo Kiev?

21 In the second leg, Villa won 2-0 with a terrific solo effort by Gary Shaw and a header from which defender?

22 Who were Villa's kit manufacturers during this season?

23 Which team did Villa meet in the European Cup Semi-Final?

24 Villa played the home tie first, who scored the only goal of the game?

25 Before the second leg, Villa played and won three league games including two 3-0 wins over which South Coast teams?

26 Villa drew the second leg of their European Cup Semi-Final 0-0. How many of their starting eleven that day began the Final against Bayern Munich?

27 After a return to form over recent matches, Villa slumped to a surprising, midweek home defeat losing 4-1 to which club who were relegated at the end of the season?

28 In May, Villa won 1-0 at The Hawthorns. Which future Villa player was sent off for WBA?

29 Villa ended the domestic season with a 3-0 home victory. It was played on a Friday night so as to avoid the FA Cup final the following day. Who did Villa beat?

30 The European Cup Final of 1982 was held at the stadium of which club?

31 In the final, Nigel Spink replaced Jimmy Rimmer after only 9 minutes. In what way did their kits clearly differ? A: Spink's shirt did not have the black contrast sleeves that Rimmer's had, B: Spink wore white shorts while Rimmer wore black, C: Rimmer wore a long sleeve jersey while Spink had short sleeves, D: Rimmer wore black socks while Spink wore white?

32 What number was on Spink's shirt?

33 The famous goal TV commentary that is celebrated on Villa Park's North Stand was spoken by who?

34 Who was the first player to reach Peter Withe after he scored the winning goal? A: Gordon Cowans, B: Gary Williams, C: Tony Morley or D: Gary Shaw

35 Which player thought they had equalised with a few minutes to go, only to find their effort ruled out for offside?

36 And which TV co-commentator for the evening called 'offside' even before the ball hit the net?

37 Which manager guided Villa through the post-Saunders months, to this European Glory??

38 As Dennis Mortimer approached to collect the European Cup trophy he was immediately followed by two players who had already swapped shirts. Who were they?

39 Villa's victory meant the European Cup had then been won by British clubs for how many consecutive years

40 In which city did the European Cup turn up at a police station a few hours after it went missing from a pub at an event organised by the club in Tamworth?

1982-83 World Cup, World Club Cup, Super Cup

1 Before a Summer break, Villa played a friendly against a team heading for their first ever World Cup Finals who were they?

2 Which two Villa players went to the World Cup in Spain?

3 The new season also bought a sponsors name to the Villa shirts. The programme for the first home game v Sunderland carried a picture of the new kit, modelled by which lady - who had been in the media at the start of the New Year because of her unscheduled appearance at Twickenham?

4 Who did Villa open their defence of the European Cup against, winning 3-1? (This was also the aggregate score for the tie)

5 What was unusual about the attendance at the home leg?

6 Which club did Ken Swain join on loan in October?

7 Villa's next tie in the European Cup started away at Dinamo Bucharest. Villa won 2-0 thanks to which player who scored both goals?

8 The same player scored a hat-trick in the return leg with a fourth added by which player scoring his first ever for the first team?

9 Because of UEFA's ruling, Villa's claret and blue jersey was different from the one worn in the football league. There were three major differences, how many can you recall?

10 Villa's growing standing in World football was boosted by an appearance against Peñarol in the World Club Championship Final. Which country were they from?

11 What was the final score?

12 By the time Villa met Liverpool a week before Christmas there was a different name as Chairman listed in the News and Record, as well as a full three page feature on the 'Man at the Helm'. Who was it?

13 After a 1-0 loss away in the first leg, Villa hosted which team in the European Super Cup?

14 Who scored late into the return game to take the tie to extra-time?

15 Which winger was fouled for Villa's penalty from which they went 2-0 up?

16 Who had his penalty saved but scored from the rebound to make it 2-0?

17 With Dennis Mortimer out of the starting line-up injured, who captained Villa and also scored their third goal?

18 How many players did Barcelona play the second half of extra time with due to their lack of discipline?

19 Which Villa player was sent off near the end of the match?

20 Which young player came on as a substitute near the end of the game for Gary Shaw and collected a gold medal on his first team debut?

21 Villa's European Cup run ended with a tie against Juventus of Italy. Can you name the 6 players who took the field at Villa Park who had played in Italy's World Cup winning team of 1982?

22 And the two other non-Italian internationals from their team who played at the 1982 tournament in Spain?

23 The home tie ended in a 2-1 loss. Who scored Villa's goal?

24 The away leg ended in a 3-1 defeat. Who scored Villa's consolation?

25 Villa qualified for the UEFA Cup as a result of their place in the Division One Table at the end of the season. Where did they finish?

Starting XI – Quiz 4

Can you name the players who kicked off the match in which Villa beat Birmingham City 5-1 on 20th April 2008?

Tenable – Quiz 4

Can you name the last 10 clubs to have played in a FA Cup Semi-Final at Villa Park ?

Number	Club
1st	
2nd	
3rd	
4th	
5th	
6th	
7th	
8th	
9th	
10th	

Map Quiz 2: European Villans

Can you match the players to the location of the nation they can represent at international level?

Fernando Nelson, Andreas Weimann, Benito Carbone, Libor Kozak
Joey Gudjonnsen, Gabor Kiraly, Phillipe Senderos, Bosko Balaban,
Kosta Nedeljkovic, Charles N'Zogbia, George Boateng, Bjorn Engels,
Thomas Hitzlsperger, Robin Olsen, Carlos Cuellar, Andy Townsend,
Aleksander Tonev, Jores Okore, John Carew, Filip Marschall, Alpay Ozalan,
Peter Enckelman

Villanagrams 3

Can you rearrange the letters to reveal more names with Aston Villa connections?

1 RED RAM PARK

2 I NO EYE BALL

3 CUP CHEER ROT

4 MACHO ALLURE

5 SUGARY TART

6 BRAZIL OK OK

7 EURO PLAUDIT

8 JEERS MATCHES

9 RETIED MOTORBOAT

10 TORN ADMISSION

11 PRAYER SHARK

12 SHOT NEAR ME SONS

13 ARDENT VERGERS

14 ENJOY AWARD

15 SHY DRAMA

16 SAVE KINDA IN

17 MESH LIKE EYE

18 DEFENDER MILK OUT

19 TARGET SOFT VEG

20 AH MINDSET

Starting XI – Quiz 5

Can you name the players who kicked off the match in which Villa beat Inter Milan 1-0 on the night and the tie on penalties? The date was 29th September 1994

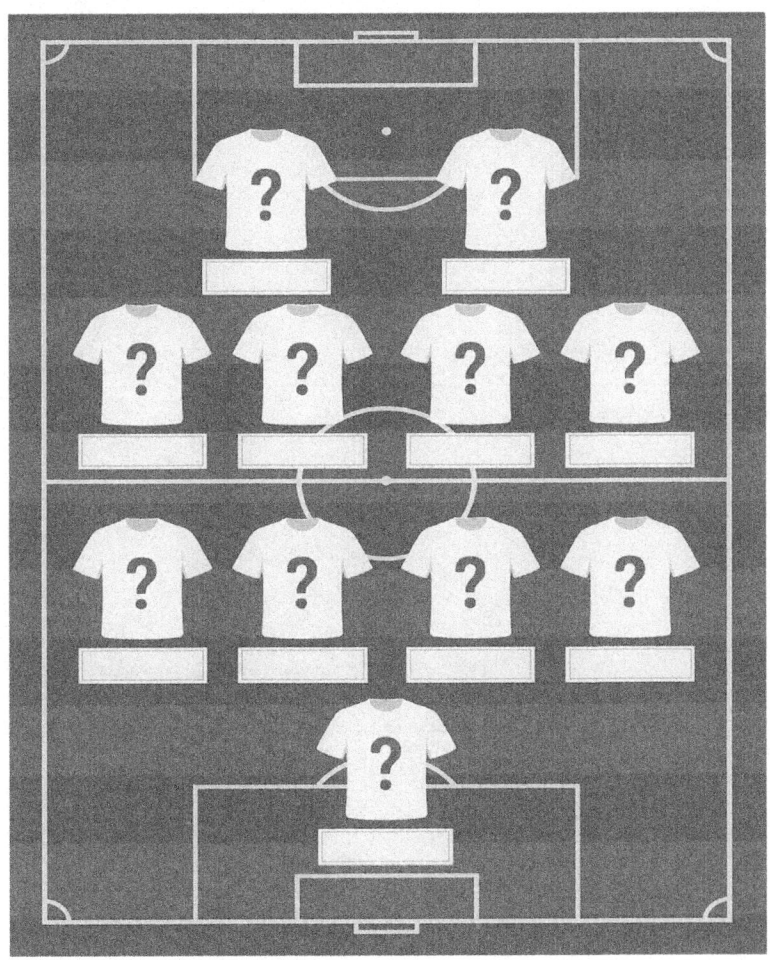

Tenable – Quiz 5

Can you name the last 10 shirt sponsors who have not been gambling companies? You might be surprised how far back this one goes!

Number	Shirt Sponsors
1st	
2nd	
3rd	
4th	
5th	
6th	
7th	
8th	
9th	
10th	

Question Set Five – A Fall and Rise and the End of the Old Divisions

1983/84 Away Day Blues

1 Which Italian side were said to be interested in signing Gordon Cowans in the close season?

2 Who did Villa pay £350,000 to secure the services of Paul Rideout

3 The opener was a thriller as Villa, now wearing claret shorts overcame West Bromwich Albion 4-3 to take top spot on 'Match of the Day'. Who made his Villa debut?

4 Which two Dutch players were in West Brom's team?

5 And which Villa favourite lined up in WBA's defence?

6 Villa made the most of two opening fixtures at Villa Park by also beating Sunderland 1-0. Who scored a terrific volley to give Villa the win?

7 David Geddis moved away in September, which club did he join?

8 Villa got through the first round of the UEFA Cup 5-1 on aggregate against which Portuguese club?

9 Another home derby, another incident packed match. Peter Withe scoring the only goal of the game at home to Birmingham City. Which Villa player was sent off?

10 Which player collided with a linesman, missed a penalty and reportedly aimed a headbutt at Steve McMahon after the final whistle?

11 The history books had long since reported the feat of Ted Drake scoring all 7 of Arsenals goals at Villa Park in the mid-1930's, but another Arsenal striker scored 5 in this season's home game, a 2-6 defeat. Who scored 5?

12 Villa went out of the UEFA Cup in cruel fashion conceding an injury time goal at home to go out on aggregate by 3-4. Which Russian side won the tie?

13 After the humiliating defeat by Arsenal, Villa won the following Saturday 2-1 at Old Trafford. Who got both Villa's goals?

14 Which club knocked Villa out of the FA Cup at the 3rd round stage, but less than a week later were beaten by Villa in a League Cup Quarter Final?

15 Which team beat Villa 2-1 on aggregate to reach the League Cup Final?

16 What 'Villa Park first' happened when Villa played Liverpool in a home match in January?

17 In March, there was another entertaining match with local rivals. A 3-3 draw with Coventry City. Which outfield player went in goal when Nigel Spink was injured?

18 Steve Foster joined Villa in an exchange deal with Brighton and Hove Albion. Which defender went the opposite way?

19 There were nine Midlands clubs in the 1st Division that season. Which one of the following teams was playing in a lower tier? A: Derby County, B: Notts County, C: Stoke City, D: Wolves

20 Of the bottom six teams at the end of the season, how many places were occupied by Midlands clubs?

1984/85 Turning to Turner

1 Villa's pre-season included a mini tournament in Barcelona. Which top West German and Argentinian clubs did they face?

2 The season began with a new manager: Graham Turner. From which lower division club did he join Villa?

3 What Villa manager record did Graham Turner beat when he took over?

4 After a good start, and wins over Coventry City and Stoke City, Villa suffered a 5-0 home defeat. Trevor Christie scored a hat trick for the visitors. Who were they?

5 In October, Villa thumped Manchester United 3-0. This marked the debut of the only close season signing from another club, Mulhouse FC. Who was the player?

6 Still in October the topsy-turvy nature of the season saw Villa concede 5 away to Leicester without reply. Who scored a hat-trick for the Foxes?

7 QPR were responsible for knocking Villa out of the League Cup. The only goal of the game came from a player who already had connections to Villa and indeed would do so once again. Who scored?

8 In mid-November, Villa threw away a home two goal lead to draw 2-2 courtesy of two goals by ex Leeds United and Scotland war horse Joe Jordan. Who was he playing for?

9 An early Christmas present saw the Villa crowd enjoy a 4-0 home win, thanks to a Paul Rideout hat-trick. Who did Villa beat?

10 In April, which 17 year old, soon to be a favourite, made his Villa debut in a 0-2 away defeat to Southampton?

11 Villa's inconsistent form rewarded them with a 10th place finish at the season end. Which legendary player was allowed to join Brighton and Hove Albion on a free-transfer?

12 And which equally important player from the 1981 Champions squad followed him out of the door to join Sheffield United?

1985/86 Low Gates

1 Villa played out a goalless draw early in the season at St Andrews. Which future international was in Birmingham's goal that day?

2 Villa beat Exeter City away in a League Cup 2nd round match 4-1. Who scored all 4 goals on his Villa debut?

3 Villa crushed Exeter at home in the second leg. What was the score?

4 After beating Leeds in the next round of the League Cup, Villa beat West Bromwich Albion in a 4th round replay. Which World Cup winner was Albion's manager?

5 After losing away to Leicester on Boxing Day, Villa's home Christmas fixture ended in a 1-1 draw with West Bromwich Albion. Which player who would go on to play for teams such as Middlesbrough and Millwall scored Villa's goal and which ex-Villa player got their equaliser?

6 Villa needed an FA Cup replay and extra time to get past which lower division opponents 3-2?

7 Villa also needed a replay to reach the semi-finals of the League Cup. Who did they beat in the quarter-final?

8 Villa played only one League match in February, a 0-0 home draw. The attendance was an astonishingly low 8,456. Who were the visiting team?

9 Villa drew the first-leg of their League Cup semi-final 2-2 at Villa Park. Who were their opponents and which Villa player scored a superb left foot volley?

10 Villa lost 3-0 at home to Birmingham City in March. Which of the 1981 Villa title winners was playing for Blues?

11 Villa pulled away from relegation, thanks to winning their last 4 home matches. One of these was their biggest league win of the season. A 4-1 victory over which club?

12 After Stoke City were relegated the season before with only 17 points, another 2 midlands teams went down this season, neither reaching 30 points. Who were they?

1986/87 The Dreaded Drop

1 Garry Thompson made his debut in the opening game of the season. Which club did he sign from?

2 Villa lost that opening match 0-3 at home, Clive Allen scoring a hat trick. Who were the opponents?

3 Villa then lost their first away game, 3-2 at Wimbledon. Which two future Villa players were on the score sheet that day?

4 After Graham Turner was sacked, who took over as caretaker manager for the home match v Norwich City?

5 The Billy McNeil era got off to a promising start with a 3-3 draw away to which club?

6 In December, Villa rallied from 3-1 down to draw 3-3 at home to Manchester United. Who scored the penalty that completed the fight back?

7 Although unawares at the time, victory over Charlton Athletic on Boxing Day was to be followed by only two more league wins in the rest of the season. Can you name either of the two teams Villa beat?

8 In January, Villa lost 3-0 at White Hart Lane. Which recently departed ex-Villan scored twice for Spurs?

9 Villa's last home game ended in a 2-1 loss to Sheffield Wednesday. Which midfielder, who made just a total of 3 appearances in his Villa career scored his only goal for the home club?

10 By the final game of the season, Billy McNeil was gone. Who took charge of Villa in their game at Old Trafford?

11 The other 2 clubs relegated with Villa that season have now both won the Premier League title. Who are they?

12 Which player, a defender, made the most appearances for Villa in this season?

1987/88 Second Division – The 'Shambles'

1 The 2nd Division season did not start well, Villa took two points from the first 12 and were beaten in their first home game. Who did they lose to?

2 Villa beat 1st Division opposition in the 3rd round of the League Cup dispatching Spurs 2-1 at home. Who scored the winner?

3 Villa exited the League Cup at the next hurdle, losing to ten-man Sheffield Wednesday. Which player had a set to with Gary Megson who was sent off?

4 Villa's form picked up to the extent that they only lost one league game between 12th September to 6th February. Who did they lose to?

5 An unremarkable home draw with Bournemouth welcomed a record for Villa as Mark Walters' goal became a milestone for total league goals scored. What were Villa the first to achieve that day? A: 4,000 goals, B: 5,000 goals, C: 6,000 goals, D: 7,000 goals

6 At the end of November, Villa hit a 4-2 win away to Bradford City. Rather strangely, two Villa players who both shared the same surname made their debuts. Who were they?

7 Villa won another match on the road in mid-December with a 2-1 win at St Andrews. Who was the Derby Day hero who scored both goals?

8 The Christmas holidays saw several draws, but Villa turned in a 5-star performance on New Years Day. Who did they thrash 5-0 at Villa Park?

9 Which Villa legend made his final appearance for Villa in a January 1-0 home win over Ipswich?

10 Villa were back on live TV for a battling 4th round FA Cup performance against 1st Division leaders Liverpool who ultimately came out 2-0 winners. Can you name either of Liverpool's scorers?

11 The last game of the season was away from home and a nerve-shredder, as Villa seeking promotion, could only play out a goalless draw. Who were the opposition?

12 Villa had a significant case of 'the wobbles' as the end of the season approached. Ultimately, they were promoted in the runners-up spot. By what margin did they finish ahead of 3rd place Middlesbrough?

1988/89 A Season of Survival

1 Which Villa Park favourite rejoined the club at the start of the season?

2 In which competition did Villa beat Birmingham City 6-0?

3 Ian Ormondroyd joined Villa during this season. From which club was he signed?

4 Which goalkeeper made his first team debut late in the season in the 1-1 away draw with Everton?

5 In their first game of December, Villa beat a team who were then league leaders and unbeaten away. Who were their opponents?

6 Which 4th Division team took a 2-0 lead at home in the FA Cup 3rd round, before a Villa revival eventually saw the away side triumph 3-2

7 Which player was the only one to start every competitive match played by Villa this season?

8 Villa only completed one league double. It was against which team (who finished rock bottom of the Division)?

9 Villa managed a point in their last game of the season, a 1-1 draw against which Midlands rivals?

10 How many places above the relegation zone did Villa end the season?

1989/90 Graham Taylor's England CV

1 Which Villa favourite moved on to join Bayern Munich before the start of the season?

2 Villa started the season at Forest with a new look defence with debuts for Kent Neilsen and which Villa legend?

3 Defender Andy Comyn made his debut this season, after signing from which local non-league club?

4 In mid-September, Villa lost to the only goal of the match scored by a player with the same surname as their manager. Who beat Villa 1-0?

5 Which rarely cautioned player was sent off after a clash with Man City's Trevor Morley as Villa won 2-0 at Maine Road?

6 On Bonfire Night 1989 Villa demolished which team 6-2 in front of a live ITV audience?

7 On Boxing Day in front of a capacity Villa Park crowd, Villa thumped Manchester United. What was the score?

8 In the first league match of the New Year, Villa beat Charlton Athletic in London. At which ground?

9 If you had SkyTV you would have been able to witness Villa live as they were beaten in the 2 legged Northern Final of the Zenith Data Systems Trophy. The winners were a team managed by Villa fan favourite, Bruce Rioch. Who were their opponents?

10 Villa's FA Cup run ended at the quarter final stage where they were soundly beaten away to a team that is currently in the National League. Who knocked them out?

11 In April, Villa won live on TV at Highbury. Which favourite full back got the 85th minute winner after brilliant work by Tony Cascarino?

12 Villa's good season ended with them as runners up in the title chase. Which team won the league?

1990/91 Scored for Villa, Never played for Villa

1 After a thrilling World Cup Finals, Graham Taylor left Villa to take the England manager's job. Who replaced him at Villa Park?

2 In their first UEFA Cup tie, Villa overcame FC Baník Ostrava and shortly revisited them to buy a player who had scored an own goal in the tie, for £500,000. He notoriously never made the Villa matchday squad in his time at the club. Who was this player?

3 In September, Villa were held to a 2-2 draw by a team who's goalscorers were Andy Sinton and Roy Wegerle. Which club were they playing for?

4 Villa produced a stellar performance on one of those unforgettable European night in the UEFA Cup home They beat eventual winners Inter Milan 2-0 at Villa Park. Which player opened the scoring that night?

5 Unfortunately Villa lost 3-0 under controversial circumstances in the San Siro to be knocked out of the UEFA Cup. Which famous German international opened the scoring?

6 In November, Derek Mountfield was sent off at Carrow Road. Which geography teaching, well known ref from Harrow produced the red card?

7 On Boxing Day, Villa drew 1-1 with Manchester United at Old Trafford. Which future Villa manager scored the home team's goal?

8 Nigel Callaghan played his last first team game for Villa during this season. He eventually transferred to Stafford Rangers but not before loan spells at 3 league clubs. Can you name any one of those?

9 In March, which forward made his Villa debut in the home defeat to Luton Town after signing from Watford?

10 Still in March, who got a hat-trick in Villa's home 3-2 win over Spurs?

11 A midweek home match with Norwich was a nervy affair as Villa sought to gain the result necessary to keep out of the relegation places. Their status was confirmed after a 2-1 win. Who scored the second vital goal?

12 Kevin Gage played his last game for Villa at the end of this season. Who did he sign for?

1991/92 Big Ron

1 What a way to begin a new season! Ron Atkinson straight back to the club he controversially left to join Villa, and a fight back after going down 2-0 to win 3-2 at Sheffield Wednesday. Who scored the winner?

2 With even more Midlands connection, who had replaced Big Ron as Wednesday's manager?

3 From which club did Villa sign Shaun Teale?

4 Still in August, which centre-back made his Villa debut, aged 18 in the 3-1 home win over Arsenal?

5 In the 4th Round of the FA Cup, Villa edged a seven goal thriller at Derby County. Dwight Yorke scored a hat-trick but which Villa full-back was shown the red card for two bookings?

6 Who scored his first Villa goal in front of the live cameras as Villa won their 5th round FA Cup tie at Swindon Town 2-1?

7 Matthias Breitkreutz was the first of two German players to make their Villa debuts this season, what was the name of the other?

8 Villa went out of the FA Cup at the Quarter Final stage 1-0 away from home. Who were their opponents?

9 In April after going behind to 2 early goals away Villa stunned the home fans by winning 5-2. Who did they beat?

10 Which goalkeeper made their Villa debut in the last away game of the season, a 2-0 loss to Luton Town?

11 In the last ever game before the Premier League, Villa beat Coventry City 2-0 at home. Who opened the scoring after just 20 seconds?

12 Ian Olney played his last game before moving to Oldham Athletic where he thrived, scoring nearly the same number of goals in half the appearances. How many goals did he score for the Villa? A: 12, B: 16, C: 20, D: 24

Question Set Six – The Premier League Era

1992-93 - The Premier League Begins

1 Who were Villa's first ever Premier League opponents?

2 With a champions' title to defend, Leeds United were attractive visitors for Villa Park's first home game of the season. A midweek crowd of over 29,000 watched. By the following Saturday when Southampton visited, things were different. Was the gate A: 17,894 B: 20,082 C: 22,517 D: 24,392

3 Who were the first team Villa defeated in the new Premier League?

4 Which Scottish striker (who scored over 130 career goals), had a short lived spell with Villa having made just 3 appearances from the bench?

5 In September, Villa put 4 past Liverpool to win 4-2. Which Liverpool player hit the bar with an open goal in front of him?

6 Into October and from a terrible miss to one of the greatest ever goals. Dalian Atkinson's chip over the goalkeeper at Wimbledon. Three players joined in to celebrate with him under an umbrella, who were they?

7 Boxing Day provided a horror show 3-0 thrashing live on TV. Which Midlands club were Villa away to?

8 In January, Villa came from a goal down to win 2-1 at Anfield. Who scored Villa's equaliser with a terrific volley?

9 Another candidate for 'best goal ever' happened in February with Dean Saunders' 40 yard volley. Who were the visitors to Villa Park?

10 And still they came! Another memorable goal to take the lead in a crucial match at Old Trafford. Who scored this thunderbolt?

11 In April, Villa drew 0-0 at home to Coventry City. Who was their keeper, who appeared to over celebrate his clean sheet?

12 Sadly, Villa's brave and exciting title challenge fizzled out as they lost their last 3 matches of the season. Can you name any of the teams they lost to? (None of them are currently Premier League clubs in the 2023/24 season)

85

Season 1993-94   Farewell Old Holte End

1 Villa got off to a great start thumping QPR 4-1 at home. They had 4 Republic of Ireland internationals in the team. Ray Houghton, Paul McGrath and Steve Staunton were joined by which player making his Villa debut?

2 At the end of August, Villa took all 3 points from Goodison Park courtesy of a single goal scored by Guy Whittingham on his full debut. Which club did Villa sign him from?

3 Villa overcame their first UEFA Cup hurdle by beating Slovan Bratislava from which country, newly independent that year.

4 Villa's journey to League Cup glory, began with a 2 leg win over who?

5 Deportivo La Coruña were Villa's next UEFA Cup opponents. Which Villa goalkeeper saved an early penalty in the first leg?

6 In the Autumn, which player was the subject of serious interest by Italian club Udinese, only for any deal to eventually fall through?

7 In the New Year, Villa beat Exeter City in the FA Cup third round. Which World Cup winner was Exeter's manager?

8 As the League Cup run continued, which pair of rival teams did Villa defeat on their own grounds in consecutive rounds? A: Southampton and Portsmouth, B: Sheffield United and Sheffield Wednesday, C: Nottingham Forest and Notts County, D: Arsenal and Tottenham Hotspur?

9 In the League Cup Semi-Final First Leg, who scored a vital last minute goal for Villa as they crumbled to a 3-1 defeat by Tranmere Rovers?

10 The second leg against Tranmere Rovers was an epic never to be forgotten. Villa scored late to level the tie, then won a penalty shoot out that went to sudden death; which five players scored penalties for Villa?

11 After a worrying drop in league form, Villa beat Manchester United in The League Cup Final. Who handled the ball to give Villa a last minute opportunity to score from the spot and make it a 3-1 scoreline?

12 The final game of the season and the final game of the Holte End standing fittingly saw Villa win 2-1 against which club?

Season 1994-95 – That Muller Sponsored Away Shirt

1 The season opener saw a 2-2 draw at Everton. Who scored on his Villa debut?

2 Villa drew with Southampton next and then again against Crystal Palace. Who denied Villa their win in the latter game scoring a late strike with less than five minutes to go?

3 Villa narrowly lost 1-0 in their first UEFA Cup match at the San Siro. Which internationally famous player scored from the penalty spot?

4 Villa thrashed Wigan Athletic 5-0 at home in their defence of the League Cup. Which teenage player who ultimately made less than 10 appearances for the club scored the first of his 3 Villa career goals (He scored the other two in the return leg)?

5 Another great European night at Villa Park. Inter Milan in the second leg. Who scored to level the tie and take it to extra time?

6 And who scored their penalties in the nail-biting shoot-out that Villa won 4-3?

7 Which goalkeeper made his debut in the return League Cup tie at Wigan where Villa won 3-0?

8 With the tie all square and in spite of playing against 10 men, Villa cruelly went out of the UEFA cup in the second round. Which Turkish club beat them on the away goals rule?

9 Ron Atkinson's last game in charge came after an away defeat where despite being 3-1 up, Villa lost 4-3. Who were the opponents?

10 Without a permanent manager, the next game was a bizarre one as Villa threw away a three goal lead away from home only to recover and score deep into injury time to emerge 4-3 victors. Who did they defeat?

11 Brian Little took over the manager's hot seat in somewhat acrimonious circumstances with the club he left. Who were they?

12 On Boxing Day and dangerously near the relegation places, Villa earned a point from a goalless draw at Arsenal. Which Villa legend made his debut after signing from Sheffield Wednesday?

13 Two days later Villa Park saw a Happy Christmas as Villa beat Chelsea 3-0. Who was Chelsea's manager that day?

14 In February, Villa demolished Wimbledon 7-1 at home. Who scored a hat-trick?

15 Villa's next home match was against Leicester City which ended in what remarkable scoreline?

16 In March, Ron Atkinson returned to Villa Park as manager of which club?

17 Because of a planned future reduction in the number of Premier League teams, how many clubs were to be relegated at the end of this season?

18 Villa found themselves staring at relegation by the time of their last home match of the season. Even a crucial 2-0 victory over Liverpool that day did not make them safe. Who scored both of Villa's goals?

19 Strangely, before their crucial, last league game, Villa beat Birmingham City in a testimonial for which player?

20 Villa assured their safety on the final day with a 1-1 draw at a club that were, themselves, relegated. Who were they?

Season 1995-96 Great Cup Runs

1 The season started with a bang, a 3-1 home win over Manchester United and the observation on Match of the Day that 'you won't win anything with kids' by which pundit?

2 Villa began their League Cup journey with a 7-1 aggregate defeat of which club?

3 Which centre back made his Villa debut in the October home win over Everton? He signed from Nottingham Forest.

4 In November, which one time Villa hero scored on his return to Villa Park as an Arsenal player in a 1-1 draw?

5 In the last game before Christmas Villa lost 1-0 to QPR at Loftus Road. Which teenager made his Villa debut from the bench only to be sent off for two yellow cards?

6 Villa were drawn away in the third round of the FA Cup, but their non-league opponents switched the tie to Villa Park. They currently play in the National League as Ebbsfleet, but what were they known as then?

7 On a very snowy weekend Villa won their 4th round FA Cup tie at Sheffield United with a cheeky penalty kick by Dwight Yorke. Which Villa legend played for the Blades that day?

8 Although a domestic competition, Villa won their League Cup Semi Final tie on the away goals rule. Who did they beat?

9 In March, Villa had a horror showing in front of the TV cameras at Anfield. How many minutes did it take for them to find themselves 3-0 down? A: 8, B: 11, C: 14, D: 17

10 Who opened the scoring against Leeds United in the 3-0 League Cup final win with a magnificent thunderbolt shot?

11 After years upon years upon years of waiting, a whole generation of Villa supporters finally saw them reach an FA Cup Semi Final. Sadly they lost. At which neutral venue were they beaten by Liverpool?

12 In what league position did Villa end the season?

Season 1996-97 Consistently Consistent

1 Which Serbian international joined Villa for the start of the new season?

2 And Nigel Spink left Villa Park to join which local rivals?

3 After making a very good start in the league, Villa went out of the UEFA Cup at the first hurdle. Which Swedish club knocked them out on the away goals rule?

4 The return leg in Sweden saw the final appearance of which Villa icon when he came on from the bench?

5 Villa were on the wrong end of a 4-3 defeat away to Newcastle in September. Who scored all Villa's goals to notch himself a hat-trick albeit in vain?

6 In the last game before Christmas, Villa handed out a 5-0 hammering which, in part, was some revenge for the recent League Cup exit at these opponents' hands. Who did they thrash?

7 Villa won their FA Cup 3rd round replay against Notts County 3-0. Which then future England manager was in charge of the visitors?

8 In March, the Villa Park crowd saw Liverpool beaten 1-0. Three future Villa players played for Liverpool that day. Can you name them?

9 In their last away match of the season, Villa lost 3-2 to a last minute penalty at Middlesbrough. Which Italian international scored from the spot?

10 A crucial 3 points were earned against Southampton in the final game of the season to cement Villa's participation in the following season's UEFA Cup. In what league position did they finish?

Season 1997-98 UEFA Cup Run

1 By the end of this season, the same two players to make the most starts in 97/98 would be precisely the same two who achieved that feat the season before. One was Ugo Ehiogu, who was the other?

2 Villa started terribly and were bottom of the division after 4 games. This included a 4-0 hammering at home by Blackburn Rovers. Which future Villa player scored a hat-trick in that match?

3 Villa safely negotiated their first UEFA Cup tie thanks to an extra time winner from Savo Milosevic. Who were their French opponents?

4 After beating Athletico Bilbao in the UEFA Cup, Villa progressed to a 3rd round tie against Steaua Bucharest. They lost the first leg 2-1 but won the home one 2-0 to reach the quarter finals. Who scored the crucial 85th minute second goal?

5 Boxing Day saw a battering for Spurs as Villa won 4-1. Two players scored two goals for Villa, one was Mark Draper, who was the other?

6 On a disastrous January day, Villa lost 5-0 at Ewood Park. Which future Villa manager opened the scoring for Blackburn Rovers?

7 Villa had shown promise in the FA Cup but were shocked in a 5th round home defeat to a team that had never won at Villa Park. Who beat Villa?

8 The John Gregory era began with a 2-1 home win over Liverpool. Which future Villa player was in Liverpool's goal?

9 John Gregory's first defeat was a shock 1-0 loss at home to a team that were having their only season in the Premier League. Who were they?

10 Villa went out of the UEFA Cup on the away goals rule but the large attendance at Villa Park did witness a memorable quality goal from Stan Collymore. Which team went to the semi-finals at Villa's expense?

11 The last away game of the season saw a 3-1 defeat of Sheffield Wednesday. Which 17 year old made their Villa debut as a substitute coming off the bench to replace Ian Taylor?

12 Villa's last eight league matches yielded seven wins, the only defeat was again at the hands of a soon to be relegated club. Which team interrupted the winning streak?

Season 1998-99 A Season of Two Halves

1 Which player joined Villa in the close season, only to be permanently transferred out of the club the very same day?

2 The first home game saw a 3-1 defeat of Middlesbrough. Which midfielder, signed from Bolton Wanderers scored on his home debut?

3 Strømsgodset IF were Villa's first UEFA Cup opponents. They shocked Villa Park, going two goals up, only for Villa to rally in the final ten minutes to win 3-2. Which player scored his first goals for the Villa?

4 Villa were more comfortable in the away leg where they won 3-0 in Norway. Which Italian made his only Villa appearance in that match?

5 Top of the table and with an away win in Spain, John Gregory decided to shuffle the pack ahead of the League Cup tie at Chelsea and Villa were thumped 4-1. Their Player/Manager scored three times, who was he?

6 Hot on the heels came another disappointing cup exit as Villa were beaten 3-1 at home in their UEFA cup second leg against which Spanish team?

7 In the first week of November, Villa beat Spurs at home 3-2. Which new signing made his Villa debut and scored 2 goals?

8 The same player went one further in the next match scoring a hat-trick in a 4-1 win away to a side who would finish one place above the relegation spots. Who were the opponents?

9 In December, after falling two behind by half time, Villa rallied to win 3-2 at home to which title rivals?

10 Boxing Day was a miserable affair losing late on to Blackburn Rovers at Ewood Park and with Michael Oakes sent off. Which goalkeeper replaced him from the bench in his one and only first team appearance for Villa?

11 Villa suffered a catastrophic loss in form in the New Year as their title aspirations faded. This was exemplified by a 4-1 home defeat to Coventry City. Which future Villa midfielder scored 2 for the Sky Blues?

12 Eventually, Villa ended back on a winning run of matches in April, but they lost their last game at home to soon to be relegated Charlton Athletic by 3 goals to 4. Which Villa player had scored at both ends before the eighth minute?

Season 1999-2000 – At Last, an FA Cup Final

1 Villa began with a 1-0 win at St James' Park which also saw the dismissal of which Newcastle player on his 100th appearance for the club?

2 In October, which returning player was sent off for Liverpool as they played out a goalless draw at Villa Park?

3 Villa's FA Cup run began earlier than usual, in December with a third round tie against a team that had already been beaten in the previous round. Who were the 'Lucky Losers' that lost 2-1 at Villa Park?

4 The last match before Christmas saw Villa beat Sheffield Wednesday 2-1 in spite of missing two penalties. However the match may be more likely remembered for a worrying neck injury to which Villa player?

5 Villa were knocked out of the League Cup, only to be re-instated as their opponents fielded an ineligible player. Who did they beat 3-1 in the re-staged quarter-final?

6 Having scored a brilliant long range goal in the FA Cup third round, which mercurial player went even further in Round 5 with a stunning 35 yard goal as part of his hat-trick as Villa beat Leeds 3-2?

7 Villa reached the semi finals of the League Cup. Which club denied them an appearance in the final?

8 Villa booked an FA Cup Semi Final place after winning away to which team in the last eight?

9 Young striker Richard Walker made the majority of his 10 Villa appearances during this season, scoring 2 Premier League goals, both at home. His first was against Watford. Who did he score his other goal against?

10 Villa played out a goalless draw in their FA Cup semi final at Wembley. Who were their opponents?

11 Still with the same match, Villa were reduced to 10 men during the extra time period. Which player was sent off?

12 The semi-final went to penalties and Villa won the shootout 4-1. Who scored the 4 penalties?

13 In mid-April, after going 2-0 down early in the second half, Villa scored 4 goals without further reply in 12 minutes to win at which London club?

14 Villa finished their league campaign with a 1-0 home defeat to Manchester United. What position did Villa achieve in the division?

15 The last FA Cup Final at the old Wembley Stadium saw Villa lose 1-0 to a goal scored by a future Villa manager. Which team did they lose to and who scored their winner?

Season 2000-01 Gallic Flair

1 The Villa player who would pick up the most yellow cards in this season, signed for a fee of around 8 million from Fenerbahçe. Who was he?

2 What was David Ginola's squad shirt number?

3 Villa made it to the semi-final stage of the Intertoto Cup, losing to Celta Vigo. In the previous round they beat FK Příbram from the Czech Republic. Where did Villa play both of their home ties?

4 Which new striker unfortunately saw their Villa and football career end almost as soon as it started with a terrible injury at Ipswich Town?

5 There were to be no long excursions into the domestic cups. Villa lost their 3rd round home tie in the League Cup to a last minute Kevin Horlock penalty. Who was he playing for?

6 Another Bonfire Night, another televised win over Everton. This time at Goodison Park. Who scored a last minute, 35 yard beauty to win 1-0?

7 In December, Villa drew at home to Manchester City 2-2 despite losing a player to his second red card of the season. Who was sent off?

8 Gilles De Bilde returned to his parent club after a short loan spell. Which country did he represent at international level?

9 The last home game of the season was a cracker, both for how it went, and also for the importance to the opponents: Coventry City who needed a win to keep hopes alive of avoiding relegation. They took a two goal lead by virtue of a brace by which player who would shortly join Villa?

10 Late in the same game Villa equalised courtesy of the first Villa goal by which January signing?

11 And who scored Villa's winner in the 86th minute to make the result a 3-2 Villa win?

12 Which striker who had served Villa greatly in 6 seasons, scoring 44 goals, joined Coventry at the end of the season?

Season 2001-02 Graham Taylor Part 2

1 Once again, Villa entered the Intertoto Cup, this time winning a final after beating FC Basel. Which French club did they beat in the Semi-Finals?

2 Having made the tortuous journey to the UEFA Cup 1st round, Villa threw it away, losing on away goals to Varteks. Which country are they from?

3 The opening fixtures were challenging. After draws with Spurs and Manchester United, Villa travelled to Anfield and won 3-1. Which future Villa employee scored for Liverpool only to later receive a straight red card?

4 Villa made an impressive start with their first league defeat not coming until deep into October. What was unusual about their last minute consolation goal in a 3-2 loss at Everton?

5 At the end of October, Villa reached top spot in the table. This followed a 3-2 home win over which team? (They featured ex player Gareth Farrelly in the starting line up and ex goalkeeper Kevin Poole on the bench)

6 Who officially opened the new Trinity Road Stand in November?

7 Villa were knocked out of the League Cup at home to Sheffield Wednesday. Making a rare start was striker Boško Balaban, a £7 million plus signing from which Croatian club?

8 After going top of the table, Villa only won a further 6 matches for the rest of the season. In January, despite being as high as 7th in the table, John Gregory resigned as manager. Who took interim charge alongside Stuart Gray for Villa's home game with Everton?

9 Graham Taylor's first win back in charge was a last gasp home victory over West Ham. Which 19 year old German was handed his first start?

10 In April 2002, which newly signed striker scored on his debut in a 1-1 draw at home to Newcastle United?

11 Villa then lost away to Middlesbrough. Which two ex players scored against the Villa in a 2-1 defeat?

12 Villa won the FA Youth Cup beating a side that included Wayne Rooney 4-2 on aggregate in the final. Who did they defeat?

Season 2002-03 A "Lousy" Season

1 Once again, Villa tried the Intertoto Cup route but lost in the Semi-Final stage to which French team?

2 The first league game of the season, a 1-0 defeat at home to Liverpool saw Ulises de la Cruz make his Villa debut. Which club did he sign from and which country did he play international football for?

3 A long awaited second city derby came around quickly in September. A delighted St Andrews crowd enjoyed a 3-0 win. This included, 'that goal from that throw in'. Which goalkeeper let the ball run under his foot into the net?

4 And who took 'that throw in'?

5 And which referee let the goal conceded from 'that throw in' stand?

6 Villa had better luck in December, beating West Bromwich Albion at Villa Park 2-1. However they had to wait until the 90th minute for a spectacular winning goal scored by which player?

7 After beating Preston North End 5-0 in the previous round, Villa went out of the League Cup at home 4-3 in the Quarter Final. With a big TV audience watching, the match was embarrassingly delayed for 80 minutes due to 'ticketing problems'. Who beat Villa?

8 There was some Christmas cheer on 28th December with a 1-0 home win over Middlesbrough. Which current Premier League manager (as of April 2024) made his Villa debut?

9 Blackburn Rovers came to Villa Park for the 3rd round of the FA Cup and beat their hosts 4-1. Which former Villa player scored twice in the game?

10 At the end of the month, new signing, Joey Guðjónsson scored on his debut in a 5-2 away win against which club?

11 In February, Villa lost 2-1 away at Fulham. At which ground did this match take place?

12 A much anticipated chance for revenge on Birmingham City evaporated in March as Villa lost 2-0 at home. Dion Dublin was sent off for a 'headbutt' on which player?

13 Villa ended the game with 9 men, who else was dismissed?

14 Villa eased concerns of relegation by winning their last two home games against Chelsea 2-1 and Sunderland 1-0. Which striker scored all 3 of Villa's goals?

15 True/False? Juan Pablo Angel scored more goals in domestic cup competitions than in this entire league season?

Season 2003-04 Looking Upward

1 Before the new season began, Villa had another new manager. Who took over at Villa Park,?

2 Villa's first win of the new season came in style with them 3 goals up after just 15 minutes. The scoreline at Villa Park ended 3-1 with Les Ferdinand sent off for the visitors. Who were their opponents?

3 Villa were disappointed with a 1-1 draw at home to Bolton Wanderers. Goalkeeper Thomas Sørensen was forced off with an injury leaving his replacement to play the second half. Who was the substitute goalkeeper?

4 After seeing off Wycombe Wanderers, Leicester City and Crystal Palace, Villa booked a League Cup Semi-Final with a 2-1 win at home to which fellow Premier League club?

5 The draw for the 3rd round of the FA Cup took on a familiar guise with Villa being paired again with Manchester United. After taking the lead at home, Villa went out 2-1 courtesy of two goals scored by who?

6 The first leg of the League Cup semi final was a thriller, but ultimately a disaster as Villa went down 5-2 at which opponents?

7 In the second leg, just 6 days later Villa won 2-0 to fall a goal shy of levelling the tie. Their task was not helped after being reduced to ten men. The player who saw red would eventually leave Villa to join the opposition club. Who was the player?

8 The January transfer window saw more players leaving than arriving. In fact only one was incoming: Nolberto Solano. Who did he represent at international level?

9 After a goalless draw at St Andrews earlier in the season, Villa drew again in the return in February, frustratingly throwing away a 2 goal lead to be pegged back in the 4th minute of injury time. Which young striker made his Villa debut from the subs bench?

10 Easter Monday saw a terrific performance rewarded with a 3-2 home win over high flying Chelsea. Juan Pablo Angel was the regular penalty taker, but who scored from the spot in this match?

11 Throughout the season, Villa's defence often included a Dane, a Swede and which Norwegian, who departed at the end of this season?

12 After an uncertain start, Villa finished the season strongly, and were in contention for a Champions League place. As it was, they ended in sixth position, losing a UEFA Cup spot on goal difference to which club?

Season 2004-05 Narrowly Missing Out

1 Which legendary defender made his Villa debut in the opening game, a 2-0 victory at home to Southampton?

2 Villa's only victory in the domestic cups came with a 3-1 home win over Queens Park Rangers. Which French midfielder signed in the Summer from Nantes made his debut?

3 December was miserable with only one point gained. This came after a fight back at home to a side who had taken the lead through Harry Kewell. Who did Villa draw with 1-1?

4 Another favourite FA Cup pairing, this time with the Blades sent Villa to Bramall Lane in front of the TV cameras. What division were Sheffield United playing in when they beat Villa 3-1?

5 The end of the January transfer window heralded a 1-1 draw away to Fulham as Juan Pablo Angel wasted two penalty kick opportunities. Villa's only new signing made his debut appearance off the bench? Who was this substitute?

6 No points this season from matches against Birmingham City. After a defeat at home early on, Villa left with nothing from St Andrews after a 2-0 loss. Which future Villa player opened the scoring?

7 The derby defeat was followed by the strangest of matches at Newcastle United. Who scored twice from the penalty spot in Villa's 3-0 win?

8 Which Newcastle player was sent off for a handball that led to one of the penalties?

9 Which two Newcastle players were sent off for fighting each other?

10 Who was Newcastle's manager who organised a hasty press conference after the game?

11 Thomas Sørensen made the most league appearances with a total of 36. Which outfield player, a defender, was the next highest with 34?

12 Villa's highest league goal scorer of the season, managed a mere total of 8 Who was it?

Season 2005-06 'We're Not Fickle'

1 The season opener was a strange affair where all 4 goals were scored before the first ten minutes. Which well-travelled goalscoring machine scored on his Villa debut in the 2-2 draw with Bolton Wanderers?

2 The first win of the season came at home to Blackburn Rovers. Milan Baroš, scoring the only goal of the game on his debut. Which Czech compatriot also made his Villa debut?

3 James Milner made his Villa debut in September. How old was he?

4 The League Cup tie away to Wycombe Wanderers looked to be heading for disaster as Villa left the field at half-time 3-1 down. What was the final score?

5 In October, David O'Leary celebrated a 1-0 victory at St Andrews by crossing the pitch to acknowledge who?

6 In the third round of the League Cup, Villa beat the club who had knocked them out last season. Who did they defeat?

7 However, the next round saw a humiliating loss in front of the TV cameras as Villa lost 3-0 away at which League One team?

8 After dismantling Everton 4-0 at home on Boxing Day, Villa drew 3-3 at Fulham. Which defender scored twice for Villa?

9 Eirik Bakke returned to his parent club after a loan spell that saw 14 appearances. Which club loaned him out?

10 In February, Villa enjoyed another 4-0 win, this time at the Riverside to see off Middlesbrough? Who scored a hat-trick?

11 After getting to the 5th Round of the FA Cup, a quarter final place looked likely until Manchester City equalised in the last minute. Which future Villa player scored the equaliser and how old was he?

12 And which ex Villa player scored the deciding goal in the replay in a 2-1 loss?

13 In March, still in the lower end of the table, Villa drew 0-0 at home to Fulham. Complete the message on the banner? 'We're not fickle…..'

14 Some relief came in April with a double over Birmingham City, this time 3-1. Apart from the win, this match was memorable for 'that goal'. Who scored Villa's goal of the season with the teams tied at 1-1?

15 Who was Villa's back up goalkeeper who made 2 appearances and was an unused sub 43 times that season?

Season 2006-07 Sir Doug Sells!

1 All change! Which team was the first to be beaten in a league match by a Villa side managed by Martin O'Neill?

2 Stilyan Petrov made his debut in September after signing from where?

3 In the League Cup 2nd round, Villa won 2-1 at Glanford Park. Who were their opponents?

4 Which French winger left Villa in November having made 6 appearances from the bench, his debut being as recent as October?

5 In December, Villa's injuries to goalkeepers necessitated an emergency short term loan for Gábor Király. Which club was his parent club?

6 December was a miserable time results wise, some cheer was around 2 days before Christmas, even though the match ended in a 3-0 home defeat to the regular winter visitors from Old Trafford, as which Villa legend took to the pitch at half time, the first time he had returned in twenty years?

7 Well, there's a surprise! Villa were drawn with Manchester United in the 3rd round of the FA Cup. A decent enough away performance was also seen by a TV audience, but Villa lost 2-1 to an injury time goal by Ole Gunnar Solskjær. Which striker scored Manchester United's first goal on his debut?

8 Villa finally found some form in January to beat Watford 2-0. This home game proved to be the last Villa appearance for Jlloyd Samuel. Which club did he join later in the year?

9 Which player made his Villa debut away to Newcastle on the last day in January, having arrived in a swap deal with Milan Baroš going to Olympique Lyonnais?

10 With the end of the season in sight, Villa beat Manchester City away 2-0. Which recent signing scored Villa's second with a great free-kick?

11 Villa's final home game saw the return of the 1982 squad to rapturous applause, before a 3-0 win against a team who were to be relegated the following week in agonising fashion. Who did Villa beat?

12 Complete the slogan on those free scarves: 'Proud History......'?

Season 2007-08 Olof's Farewell

1 Nigel Reo-Coker made his debut in the opening game of the season, a 2-1 home defeat to Liverpool. Which club was he signed from?

2 Another player from the same club also made his debut in August as Villa beat Fulham 2-1. Who is he?

3 The second round of the League Cup saw Villa win 5-0 in Wales. Who did they beat?

4 September saw the TV cameras catch a very happy Doug Ellis shaking hands with Roman Abramovich as the latter left early as Villa secured a great 2-0 win over Chelsea. Who began the scoring on his Villa Park debut?

5 Once again on TV as the Villa fans sang 'Happy Birthday to you' while 4-1 up at a 125th anniversary celebrating Tottenham Hotspur at White Hart Lane. Incredibly, the match ended 4-4. Which defender scored the last, injury time goal?

6 Who got the winner when Villa beat Birmingham City 2-1 at St Andrews?

7 In December, Villa lost 3-1 at home. A main contribution was 2 stunning goals by Sulley Muntari. Which team was he playing for?

8 Boxing Day saw another amazing 4-4 draw. Which ground witnessed this game that also saw three red cards issued?

9 You're ahead of me aren't you? Yes it's FA Cup 3rd Round and it's a 2-0 loss to surprise, surprise; Manchester United. United fielded 8 different nationalities in their starting 11. How many can you name?

10 In April, a 6-0 win away at Pride Park saw 'that wonder goal' from Stiliyan Petrov. Whereabouts in the scoring sequence did it come?

11 Hot on the heels of Derby, another derby. This time a demolition derby as Villa thrash Birmingham City at home 5-1. Which players helped themselves to two goals each?

12 Olof Mellberg played his final game in Villa's final game of the season before leaving for Juventus. What grand gesture did he make to the 3,000 + travelling fans who went to Upton Park?

Season 2008-09 England Call Ups

1 Another season, another go at qualifying via the Intertoto Cup. Firstly overcoming Odense, then Fimleikafélag Hafnarfjarðar from which country?

2 Gabriel Agbonlahor helped himself to a hat-trick at Villa Park in the first league match of the new season. Who did Villa beat 4-2?

3 Which one time loan player returned to Villa permanently, making his debut in the home goalless draw with Liverpool?

4 Litex Lovech were the next team to be beaten in the UEFA Cup proper. Which country were they representing?

5 Great European nights were fully back on the menu in October as Villa beat which Dutch team 2-1 in the Group Round of the competition?

6 After some inconsistent results, Villa won 2-0 against Arsenal at the Emirates. The home side fielded six players of which nationality in their starting line-up?

7 Martin O'Neill had not been afraid to rotate the team as Villa challenged in different competitions. They came a cropper at home to QPR to exit the League Cup and were undone again in their second home European clash with which team from Slovakia who beat them 2-1?

8 A December TV treat from Goodison Park saw Villa win 3-2, scoring in the first and also the last minute. Which two players scored those goals?

9 Another televised game, the final one of 2008 saw Craig Gardner celebrate passionately as the referee changed his decision to award Villa's hosts a last minute penalty. Who did Villa beat 1-0?

10 Which new signing in the January window scored the only goal of the match on his debut as Villa won at Portsmouth?

11 Back to knockout matches in the UEFA Cup round of 32. After a 1-1 home draw, Martin O'Neill fields a much changed and inexperienced side in the away leg and Villa disappointingly go out, beaten 2-0. Who beat them?

12 In the next match Villa threw away a 2-0 lead in the last 4 minutes against which Midland rivals?

13 Things did not improve in the following matches and Villa were thumped 5-0 at Anfield. A game not helped by the dismissal of a Villa player who had previously been with Liverpool. Who got their 'marching orders'?

14 Villa lost their next match 3-2 at Old Trafford, the winning goal coming deep in injury time by which 17 year old making his debut from the bench? (I can still hear Martin Tyler's commentary, unfortunately).

15 Which team lost 1-0 to Villa in the last match of the season and were relegated?

Season 2009-10 Wembley Double

1 Villa exited Europa League competition almost as quickly as they started, going out at the first hurdle to which team on away goals?

2 A rare thing indeed, Villa got a penalty at Anfield and win 3-1. A much needed result after the opening day home defeat to which team?

3 Happy times in September as Villa won at St Andrews 1-0. No less than 3 defenders made their debuts for Villa in the match. How many can you name?

4 Villa got past Sunderland in the 4th Round of the League Cup thanks to penalty shootout heroics in the Stadium of Light from Brad Guzan. How many did he save?

5 Not only a penalty at Anfield, but now a win at Old Trafford! Who scored the only goal?

6 After beating Blackburn Rovers in the FA Cup, Villa travelled to….. Blackburn Rovers in the first leg of the League Cup semi final. They went back to Villa Park with a lead courtesy of the only goal of the game scored by who?

7 The second leg was a ridiculous roller coaster of a match. Villa won, and booked a Wembley place, but what was the score on the evening?

8 In the League Cup final, which referee decided not to send Manchester United's Nemanja Vidic off after he conceded an early penalty?

9 Villa went back to Wembley for an FA Cup Semi-Final. Once again there was controversy over the referee's decision to only give John Terry a yellow card for his challenge on James Milner and also his refusal to award what clearly looked like a penalty kick earlier in the game. Who was the referee?

10 Late in the season, Villa beat Birmingham City at home, taking their league haul of points to 13 from the last five matches since they were hammered in the league at Stamford Bridge. How many had Chelsea put past Villa in that catastrophic match?

Season 2010-11 Out of the Blue?

1 Martin O'Neill walked out on Villa on the eve of the new season. Who did Villa meet in their opening, manager-less game?

2 Once again, Villa exited European competition at the first hurdle, and to the same team that put them out last year. Ironically this was the club from whom Villa had signed a striker who was to make his debut in the season opener. Who was he?

3 James Milner left to join Manchester City. Which player came the other way as part of the deal?

4 Villa finally appointed a permanent manager who was not available to take immediate charge. It was not until a League Cup match late in September that he took control. Who was the new manager?

5 There was a fair bit of fuss when Villa beat Blackpool 3-2 at home, as the visitors had made ten changes to their starting XI. Who was the Blackpool manager?

6 After a miserable pair of Christmas results, Villa drew 3-3 at Stamford Bridge. Lee Mason booked 7 Villa players. Who scored Villa's injury time equaliser?

7 Which player, who's father at the time was the USA national team coach, joined Villa on loan and made 4 appearances?

8 Yes, it's FA Cup 3rd round time again with more evidence that if Manchester United aren't going to be Villa's opponents, then it's highly likely to be Sheffield United. Which player scored on his loan debut for Villa against his boyhood club in a 3-1 Villa away win?

9 Villa's patchy form continued with some relief coming with a 1-0 win over Manchester City. Who scored the only goal on his home debut?

10 Which player who preferred to be differentiated from his father by having II between his given name and surname, joined Villa in the January window, received a straight red after only a handful of games at Blackpool

and eventually left the club in 2013 after making just 11 first team appearances?

11 In April, Villa eased their relegation worries with two successive wins, beating Newcastle 1-0 and then West Ham 2-1. Who got Villa's injury time winner at Upton Park?

12 Villa were able to stop 'looking over their shoulders' after the penultimate match which was a victory away at Arsenal, they then ensured a barely believable 9th place finish after a final day 1-0 win over Liverpool. Who scored Villa's goal that day?

Season 2011-12 In From the Blues!

1 Somewhat amazingly, Villa appointed Alex McLeish as manager. During this season, two Scottish players appeared for Villa, one a new signing. Who were they?

2 In the League Cup second round, Villa beat a League Two side who would shortly be relegated to non-league and not long after that be wound up. A phoenix team now plays under a very similar name in the Vanarama National League North. Who were they?

3 Lots of drawn games were a feature of the early part of the season, but Bonfire Night saw a 3-2 win at home to Norwich City. Which current TV presenter made his delayed Villa debut in this match?

4 On New Year's Eve, Villa picked up an unlikely but welcome 3-1 win on the road. Their opponents at the time were managed by André Villas-Boas. Who did Villa beat?

5 In January, which new short-term signing scored twice against old club Wolves in a 3-2 win at Molineux?

6 In March, Villa grabbed all three points at home with an injury time winner to beat Fulham 1-0. It was the first Premier League goal for which striker, who later referred to it as his 'crab goal'?

7 At Easter, Villa drew 1-1 at Anfield, after taking the lead through Chris Herd. What nationality is he?

8 Villa finished the season in 16th place 3 points ahead of the relegation places. How many games did they win during the season? A:5, B:7, C:9 or D:11

9 Carlos Cuéllar left at the end of the season. Which club had he joined Villa from?

10 Defender James Collins also left in the close season, who did he sign for?

Season 2012-13 The Wheels Start to Come Off

1 Villa got off to a poor start losing both of their opening games. Can you name either opponent?

2 Villa's first win was at home to Tranmere Rovers in the League Cup. Which Alex McLeish signing made his full debut in this game?

3 In September, Villa won unexpectedly, away to Manchester City in the League Cup. The score after 90 minutes was 2-2. What was the final score?

4 After throwing away a 2 goal lead to lose at home to Manchester United, Villa, then played at Manchester City once more. Villa were soundly thumped 5-0. Which striker, signed from Chesterfield made his Villa debut?

5 Villa's worrying form took a small turn for the better in early December. They beat Norwich City 4-1 away to progress to a League Cup semi final. In the Norwich team that day was which Scotland international who would become a regular feature of Villa's efforts to rise from the Championship?

6 More unexpected results were to follow. The next being a 3-1 victory at Anfield. Who scored two for Villa?

7 Riding a wave of positivity from the Liverpool game. Villa went to Stamford Bridge just before Christmas and were humiliated by what score?

8 At least Villa had an opportunity to get to a Wembley final when they were drawn against League Two opponents in the Semi-Finals of the League Cup. However, they were beaten over 2 legs 4-3. Which team knocked Villa out?

9 Villa picked up some much needed points in a 3-1 win at Stoke City. Which defender scored a sensational goal to put Villa ahead 2-1?

10 The televised home game with Sunderland provided some well needed relief as Villa won by 6 goals to 1. Which defender opened the scoring for Villa very early in the game?

11 After that Villa won at Carrow Road. Which Australian made his final Villa appearance, even though he had only spent 1 season with the club?

12 In the last game of the season, Villa drew 2-2 with which club who were relegated but also unusually that season's FA Cup winners?

Season 2013-14 Lamentable Lambert, Consistently Poor, Inconsistently 'Excellent'

1 A great start to the season as Villa, in that strange white and purple kit, upset 60,000 Gooners with a 3-1 win at the Emirates. Who scored on his debut?

2 Villa went out of the League Cup at an early stage with a whimper losing 4-0 at home to Tottenham Hotspur. Jan Vertonghen, was, however lucky not to concede a penalty for a challenge that caused a Villa player to end with his shorts round his knees. Who was the player?

3 Another significant memory shortly followed, this time of Andreas Weimann celebrating his winner in front of the Holte End. Who opened the scoring for Villa in their 3-2 win over Manchester City?

4 And who scored a beautiful free kick for Villa's second?

5 The traditional Boxing Day fixture proved miserable as Villa lost at home 1-0. The scorer was Dwight Gale in injury time. Who were Villa playing?

6 FA Cup 3rd round day and it's.......Sheffield United again. This time beating Villa at Villa Park 2-1. Which future England captain was in their line-up?

7 At the end of January in a memorable game, Villa welcomed West Bromwich Albion and were 2 down in the first ten minutes. What was the final score?

8 Which team did Villa beat at home 4-1 thanks to an own goal and a Christian Benteke hat-trick?

9 Villa gained an important win to guarantee safety at home to Hull City. Two players who would become Villa players and one who already had been with Villa took the field in Hull's defence. Can you name them?

10 Villa finished a largely miserable season losing 3-0 to Tottenham Hotspur on the TV at White Hart Lane. Who scored an own goal for Spurs' second?

Season 2014-15 'Wembley, Wembley'

1 In July, who was named Assistant Manager to Paul Lambert?

2 In September, Villa won 1-0 at Anfield. Which player signed on loan from Manchester United made his debut?

3 Between the 20th December and 1st January, Villa played 4 fixtures, Manchester United, Sunderland and Crystal Palace at home and Swansea City away. How many goals did they score in total?

4 Oddly, the FA Cup 3rd round paired Villa with neither Manchester United or Sheffield United, but which Championship team that Villa beat 1-0?

5 Villa went back to Valencia CF to sign a player for the 3rd time since the close season, this time to bring in which winger in the January window?

6 The same player scored a great goal for Villa's opener to help them win their 4th round FA Cup tie at home to which team?

7 Paul Lambert was eventually sacked in February following a loss at which relegation rivals. A loss that put Villa in the drop zone?

8 Who scored Villa's second goal to ensure victory by 2 goals to 0 in the FA Cup quarter final at home to West Bromwich Albion?

9 And which Villa player was controversially sent off in injury time for two yellow cards, the last being awarded for 'simulation'?

10 In a midweek match in April, Christian Benteke scored a hat-trick to help Villa to a 3-3 home draw against which relegation rivals?

11 Joyous scenes at Wembley as Villa beat Liverpool 2-1 to reach the FA Cup Final at …….Wembley. Who scored Villa's winner?

12 And which future Villa player scored Liverpool's only goal?

13 The final away game at St Mary's was a disaster, Villa being on the end of a 6-1 thrashing. Which Southampton forward scored a 2 mins and 56 seconds hat-trick?

14 The final league game was at Villa Park. A 40,000+ crowd attended what could have been a crucial relegation game, but Villa were safe after the

previous week's results. Just as well really as they lost to relegated Burnley 1-0. Which future Villa player scored the goal?

15 Villa lost the FA Cup Final against Arsenal 0-4. Who refereed the match?

Season 2015-16 Unforgivably Catastrophic

1 Little were we to know that an opening day win would be followed by merely two more in the entire season. Which new signing scored the only goal of the game to beat newly promoted Bournemouth?

2 No fewer than 5 players made their starting debuts for the club at Bournemouth. Of these, who was the only English player?

3 In the second round of the League Cup, Villa needed extra-time to beat Notts County at home. What was the final score?

4 September 13th was possibly the major turning point in both team's seasons as Villa visited the King Power stadium, went into a 2 goal lead with less than half an hour to go, but lost 3-2 to Title-winning bound Leicester City. Who scored Villa's opening goal?

5 Which defender made his second and final Villa appearance in the 2-1 4th round League Cup defeat away to Southampton?

6 In his first match in charge, new Villa manager Rémi Garde saw his team gain a battling goalless draw at home to which club?

7 Villa needed a replay to get past which lower league opposition in the FA Cup 3rd Round?

8 Villa's only two league wins since the opening day came at home to which clubs?

9 Rémi Garde left as manager after a 1-0 defeat away to which club?

10 Complete the slogan on the banner seen at Villa's 2-1 home defeat to Bournemouth. "No Fight, No Pride, No Effort, No ......?

Season 2016-17 Stopping the Rot

1 A new owner and a new manager. Roberto Di Matteo in the hot seat. The Italian also brings in a compatriot goalkeeper. What is his name?

2 Villa's opening game was a 1-0 defeat away to which club?

3 The first two matches at Villa Park were both against teams from Yorkshire, one who would be relegated, followed by one that would be promoted. Who were the clubs?

4 The end of August saw a 3-1 defeat at Bristol City and a tale of two strikers. One scored Bristol City's first, and would be a key asset to Villa when they were promoted back to the Premier League, the second did not play for them that day due to his impending transfer to Villa. Who are the two forwards?

5 Di Matteo made it as far as the first week in October before being replaced by Steve Bruce. He lasted 11 league games until a defeat away to Preston North End. How many wins did Villa achieve during his short tenure?

6 The Fixture Calendar threw up a rare Boxing Day derby which Villa won 2-1. The opponents were not any of the usual suspects, rather a club who had heroically won their way from Non-League football in 2009 to this, their first season in the Championship. Who are they?

7 January saw Jordan Ayew leave for Swansea City. Which player came the other way to Villa Park?

8 Towards the end of a tough first season away from the top flight, Villa beat Birmingham City at home. Who scored the game's only goal?

9 A measure of how tough Villa found their first season in the Championship is that they only completed the double over 3 teams, and two of them were relegated at the end of the season. Who was the other club?

10 What squad number did Mile Jedinak wear that season?

Season 2017-18 Last Gasp Heartbreak

1 The first win of the season was a 4-2 home win over Norwich City. Who scored a hat-trick?

2 Which player who had been recently playing non-league football made a really impressive debut in the same match?

3 The same player scored his first goal in front of the TV cameras in a 3-0 away win against which club, a win which appeared much needed by Steve Bruce at the time?

4 Villa drew 0-0 at St Andrews in October. Which future Villa player was in Birmingham City's starting XI?

5 Who did Villa trounce 5-0 at home on New Year's Day?

6 A much rotated line-up ensured a familiar early exit from the FA Cup at the first hurdle as Villa lost 3-1 at home to which League One club?

7 Villa beat Sheffield United at Bramall Lane in January. Villa fans celebrating wildly as the only goal in this televised match was scored in the 90th minute. By which player?

8 In February, Villa left it late to score two goals as they won 4-2 at Sheffield Wednesday. Who scored Villa's first goal on his first start?

9 In March, Villa smashed Championship leaders Wolverhampton Wanderers in a televised match at Villa Park. What was the final score?

10 The following week, Villa were beaten 1-0 in snowy conditions in another televised match. Steve Bruce's solution to seeking an equaliser consisted of throwing on 3 forwards from the subs bench. Who beat Villa courtesy of an Adam Le Fondre goal?

11 On the TV again! This time against promotion rivals Cardiff City. With the tension rising, the deadlock was finally broken 5 minutes from the end by a spectacular, thunderbolt volley. Who scored for Villa?

12 Villa made an appearance in the Play-Offs for the first time. What league position did they finish in?

13 The Semi-Finals were against Middlesbrough. Who was their manager?

14 Villa reached the final 1-0 on aggregate. Who scored the first-leg goal?

15 The Play-Off Final did not go Villa's way. Jack Grealish almost scored one of the greatest ever goals and was fouled repeatedly. Who was sent off for two yellow cards reducing Fulham to 10 men?

Season 2018-19 'Allez Allez Allez'

1 The televised opening match, saw Jack Grealish substituted to an ovation from the travelling fans amid genuine fears that he might join which Premier League club before the end of the transfer window?

2 It was reported that Villa were in financial trouble following their failed promotion challenge and it was a relief when new owners took over from whom?

3 After beating Wigan at Villa Park, Villa drew their next two home games, firstly with Brentford and then against Reading. Who scored an equaliser deep into injury time in the first of these and who conceded a penalty right at the end of the Reading game?

4 Villa's first defeat in the Championship came at the home of which promotion rivals who went 4 up within 50 minutes and comprehensively won 4-1?

5 Mid-September saw a tremendous strike from John McGinn worthy to win any game. Unfortunately, it didn't as Villa lost at home to Sheffield Wednesday. Which ex-Villa player started for the Owls?

6 Preston North End at home was Steve Bruce's last game in charge. Who equalised in injury time as Villa disappointedly drew 3-3, and who missed a penalty for Villa deep into stoppage time?

7 New manager Dean Smith got off to a winning start. Who did Villa beat 1-0?

8 Villa beat Birmingham 4-2 at home, who scored his much deserved wonder goal to end the scoring for the day and make the game safe for Villa?

9 A thrilling match at home to Nottingham Forest ended 5-5. What was the only scoreline when Villa were in front, during the entire match?

10 Which Villa player scored 4 goals in that game?

11 Villa were controversially held to a 2-2 draw at the Hawthorns. Who scored West Brom's injury time equaliser with his hand?

12 The New Year's Day fixture ended in a frustrating 2-2 draw with referee James Linington seemingly content to allow QPR to waste time throughout. Who was QPR's manager?

13 In February, Villa found themselves 3-0 down in the 82nd minute to a Billy Sharp hat-trick. Remarkably, they rallied to end the match with Sheffield United 3-3. Who scored the first on his home debut?

14 And who got the third against the Blades deep into added time?

15 At the start of March, Villa found themselves mid-table. What happened next was a remarkable run of ten straight wins. Who did they beat 4-0 to start this off?

16 The second win came at St Andrews. Who got the winner in a 1-0 victory?

17 Villa won 3-1 courtesy of two stoppage time goals at Sheffield Wednesday, then beat another team in Yorkshire 2-1, where both sides scored penalties, Villa also missed a penalty and played nearly an hour with 10 men. Who were their opponents?

18 Their final win in this amazing run was a 1-0 victory at home to who?

19 A 1-1 draw at Elland Road. Where to start? An injury to Jonathon Kodjia leaves him lying on the pitch. Who scored Leeds' controversial goal?

20 Who feigned to put the ball out, but didn't put the ball out, sparking the angry scenes that followed?

21 Who caused Anwar El Ghazi to receive a red card for simulating that he had been badly struck?

22 Who scored the largely uncontested equaliser straight from kick-off?

23 Villa finished the regular season with a 2-1 home defeat to the League Champions. Who were they, and who were their local rivals who finished right at the opposite end of the table?

24 The play-off semi-final went to penalties against West Brom. Who scored the 4 penalties that put Villa through?

25 John McGinn was the Wembley hero scoring the play-off Final winner against Derby County, but who opened the scoring?

Season 2019-20   VAR

1 Villa's first win was in a Friday Night TV game against Everton. Which new signing opened the scoring in a 2-0 home victory?

2 Who did Villa beat 6-1 on the road in the 2nd round of the League Cup?

3 Teething troubles understanding VAR caused Kevin Friend to deny Villa what appeared to be a legitimate goal in their next away game to which opponents?

4 Although twice in front, Villa threw away the points at Arsenal 3-2. Which future Villa player scored for the Gunners?

5 Villa presently thrashed Norwich City at Carrow Road. By what score?

6 Who did Villa beat 5-0 to progress to the Semi-Finals of the League Cup against Leicester City?

7 Villa won their semi-final tie to progress to Wembley thanks to a deep into added-on time winner in the second leg. Who scored?

8 Villa lost the League Cup Final to Manchester City. What was the score?

9 In the last Premier League game before the break due to the pandemic, Villa were thumped 4-0 away to which club?

10 In which month did 'Operation Restart' see the season recommence?

11 As the game with Sheffield United was the first after the long break, what happened prior to kick off that was soon to become widespread at football matches?

12 The goalless draw was remembered for the 'ghost goal' that was not given to the Blades as goal line technology appeared to fail. Who was the Villa goalkeeper?

13 And who was the referee?

14 The last home game of the extended season, saw Villa in deep relegation trouble, so the 1-0 win thanks to a Trézéguet goal was welcomed with relief. Who did Villa beat?

15 A very nervy point at West Ham saw Villa over the line….just. Who scored Villa's goal in the 1-1 draw?

Season 2020-21 The Strangest of Seasons

1 Villa won their opening league game 1-0. Who did they beat at Villa Park, still behind closed doors?

2 The next home match saw Villa thump reigning champions Liverpool 7-2. Can you name the 4 different Villa scorers?

3 Villa won 3-0 at the Emirates. Which player had his first minute Villa goal disallowed after a VAR review?

4 Which referee sent off Douglas Luiz, then awarded an added on time penalty which was scored to beat Wolves 1-0 at Molineux?

5 Who did Villa beat at home on Boxing Day 3-0 in spite of having to play the entire second half with 10 men?

6 The FA Cup 3rd round home tie with Liverpool broke records. Because of COVID-19 rules, Villa had to play their youth team. How many players made their first team debuts?

7 In return, Jurgen Klopp decided to field a near full strength side, maybe still thinking about that 7-2 drubbing. The match ended 4-1 to Liverpool but what was the half time score?

8 Villa lost 2-0 at the Etihad Stadium in such controversial circumstances that the laws of the game were later changed. Who was the referee on the day?

9 Villa completed the double over Arsenal with the only goal of the game coming after 2 minutes. Who scored?

10 Villa lost away to a relegation doomed Sheffield United who had to play the last half hour with ten men. Which veteran defender was sent off for the Blades?

11 Villa won their last game of the season on the road against Spurs. Which two young players made their debut in this match?

12 Jack Grealish made his last appearance (before his move to Manchester City) in the final game of the season. Who did Villa beat 2-1?

Season 2021-22 Dean and Jack Leave

1 Who scored a hat-trick in Villa's 6-0 League Cup second round win at Barrow?

2 In September, Villa won 1-0 at Old Trafford. Who scored the winning goal?

3 In mid-October, seemingly with the match under control, Villa were 2-0 up in the 80th minute. They lost this home game 3-2. To which team?

4 What was Dean Smith's last game in charge?

5 Which unlikely scorer grabbed both goals in Villa's 2-1 home win over Leicester City?

6 It's been a while, but the 3rd round FA Cup once again paired Villa with Manchester United. A 1-0 loss was even harder to take after the officials took a long, long time to rule out Danny Ings' 'equaliser'. Who was the official in charge?

7 Still in January and Villa did the double over Everton. Which caretaker manager was in charge of the home side at Goodison Park?

8 Triple teaser: At the end of February, Villa beat Brighton and Hove Albion 2-0 away. What was unusual about the kick-off time, what is the name of Brighton's stadium and which player made his Villa debut from the bench after being an unused substitute on several occasions?

9 Villa thumped Southampton 4-0 at home before winning away 3-0 at Leeds United. Who made his home managerial debut for the Yorkshire outfit?

10 After losing at home to Arsenal, Villa were beaten on their next home outing by Spurs. Heung-min Son scored a hat-trick in their 4-0 win, who got the other goal?

11 Later in April, Dean Smith returned to Villa Park for the first time. Which club was he in charge of, and what was the score?

12 In the first week of May, Villa won on their travels again with Danny Ings scoring against another of his old clubs. Who did Villa beat 3-1?

Season 2022-23 Unai Emery's Claret and Blue Army

1 Which two players made their Villa debut in the opening game away to Bournemouth?

2 Which fixture saw Villa's first win of the season?

3 In the first League Cup tie, Villa beat Bolton Wanderers 4-1 away. What was unusual about Villa's opener?

4 In September, Villa drew 1-1 at home to Manchester City, but were denied a possible winner due to an offside call not being referred to VAR. Who's goal was ruled out?

5 What was Steven Gerrard's last game in charge of Villa?

6 Which caretaker manager guided Villa to a 4-0 win over Brentford in the following match?

7 What was Unai Emery's first game in charge of Villa?

8 Villa won in the road in the final game before the break for the World Cup. Who did they beat?

9 More FA Cup misery this season with a home defeat to League Two Stevenage. Including this game, how many successive seasons had Villa gone out at the 3rd round stage?

10 During the season, Villa lost 2 consecutive home matches by 4 goals to 2. Who were the opponents?

11 At the end of February, Villa went on a 10 match unbeaten run, winning 8 of them. Which two home games did they win 3-0 during this spell?

12 Villa qualified for European competition with a final day 2-1 defeat of Brighton and Hove Albion. Who had assists for both goals?

SEASON 2023-24 Champions League Qualification

1 Who scored Villa's first goal of the season?

2 Keinan Davis left Villa to play in which country?

3 What was the aggregate score in the Europa Conference League qualifying tie with Hibernian FC?

4 In which letter Group were Villa drawn alongside Legia Warsaw, Zrinjski Mostar and AZ Alkmaar?

5 The home match against AZ Alkmaar may have followed a different path if a 3rd minute effort for Villa had not been questionably disallowed. Who's goal was not allowed to stand?

6 Who supplied the pass that allowed Leon Bailey to score the winner at home to Manchester City?

7 Who scored the goal that bought Villa's 15 home game winning run to an end?

8 Finally, Villa get through an FA Cup tie. Who scored the only goal of the 3rd round match against Middlesbrough?

9 Earlier in the season, Newcastle United had 8 different goalscorers in their 8-0 away win at Sheffield United. When Villa won 5-0 at Bramall Lane, every goal was also by a different player. Can you name them?

10 Villa's only 0-0 draw of the Premier League season came at which ground?

11 Which England international lined up against Villa in their last 16 Europa Conference League ties with Ajax Amsterdam?

12 Which referee sent off John McGinn in the home match with Tottenham Hotspur?

13 Who supplied the pass that allowed Ollie Watkins to score the second in Villa's 2-0 away win at Arsenal?

14 Who scored Villa's penalties in the shootout with Lille?

15 Which Olympiacos player scored 5 goals across the two Europa Conference League Semi-Finals against Villa?

16 And what nationality was the referee who took charge of the first leg at Villa Park? He also officiated at the Euro 2024 finals

17 Who provided the assist for the first of Jhon Duran's goals against Liverpool in the final home game of the season?

18 How many points did Villa end the season with?

19 Who was named Supporters' Player of the Season and Players' Player of the Season at the club's End of Season Awards Dinner?

20 And which goal was awarded Goal of the Season at the same Awards Dinner?

Can you name the players who kicked off the match in which Villa beat Manchester United 2-1 in the 2nd leg Semi-Final of the League Cup on 23rd December 1970?

Tenable – Quiz 6

One for the oldies! Can you name John Burridge's first 10 clubs (excluding loans).

Number	Club
1st	
2nd	
3rd	
4th	
5th	
6th	
7th	
8th	
9th	
10th	

Who Am I?

Lots of players, five clues, the sooner you guess their identity correctly, the more points you score.

Who Am I - Player 1

Clue 1: I played for a manager in Italy who had also been the manager of an English club where I spent my Youth career

Clue 2: I have winners medals in the Champions League, UEFA Super Cup and UEFA Conference League with a runner up medal in the Europa League

Clue 3: I have scored in three matches for England, the combined results of those games being 22-0

Clue 4: I had a loan spell with Swansea City

Clue 5: I scored 25 goals in a single EFL Championship season for Villa

Who Am I - Player 2

Clue1: I was bought to replace a Villa favourite who left to play in Italy.

Clue2: After Villa I had a prolific goalscoring record with a Midlands rival

Clue3: I played in a World Cup Tournament and was a pundit on ITV's coverage of The World Cup in 1974

Clue4: I served as Chairman of the Professional Footballers Association

Clue5: I played international matches in the same team as George Best

Who Am I - Player 3

Clue1: I began my career playing Gaelic Football

Clue2: The majority of my Villa appearances came in the 1950's

Clue3: I joined Villa from Leeds United

Clue4: I started out as a defender at Villa

Clue5: However I also played the major half of a season as Villa's goalkeeper

Who Am I - Player 4

Clue1: I have played for Villa, Newcastle United and Manchester City

Clue2: I have been on the books of 18 Football League clubs

Clue3: I have won the League Cup with Villa and also the equivalent in Scotland

Clue4: The club I made most appearances for was Blackpool

Clue5: My nickname is 'Budgie'

Who Am I - Player 5

Clue1: I made 62 appearances for England and scored 7 goals

Clue2: I have played at a World Cup Finals

Clue3: I have winners medals for the FA Cup, League Cup, UEFA Cup and UEFA Super Cup

Clue4: I was signed by Martin O'Neill and scored on my Villa debut

Clue5: In 2001 I played and scored in England's 5-1 win against Germany in Munich

Who Am I - Player 6

Clue1: I gained 17 international caps and scored once for my country

Clue2: I was on the books of a Manchester club but had to leave because of issues with a work visa

Clue3: I developed a reputation for saving penalty kicks

Clue4: I made over 200 appearances for Villa playing throughout most of the 1990's at Villa Park

Clue5: After Villa I played for Manchester United and Chelsea

Who Am I - Player 7

Clue1: I am a football pundit
Clue2: I had an impressive international career, including playing at two World Cups
Clue3: My first league club was Gillingham
Clue4: Ron Atkinson sold me to Glasgow Celtic
Clue5: I was, at the time, Villa's record signing, joining from Millwall

Who Am I - Player 8

Clue1: Growing up, I was an Aston Villa fan
Clue2: After Villa, I played for Leicester
Clue3: I won three caps for England
Clue4: My playing career began in the Conference with Stafford Rangers
Clue5: My middle name is Victor

Who Am I - Player 9

Clue1: Aston Villa were the club I made most career appearances for and I had a very good goal scoring record there.
Clue2: After football, I had a minor acting career
Clue3: I played for clubs in Italy, France and Turkey among other countries
Clue4: I played international football for the same team as Erling Haaland
Clue5: The Holte End sung that I'm "gonna score one or two…"

Who Am I - Player 10

Clue1: I am a former Villa captain
Clue2: I joined Villa from West Bromwich Albion
Clue3: I was a semi-finalist with my country at UEFA Euro 2016
Clue4: I was ever present in the 2017/18 Championship season
Clue5: My surname is also shared with a city in the UK

Who Am I - Player 11

Clue1: Villa was my only permanent English club although I had a brief loan spell with Derby County

Clue2: I was with Villa when they won the 1st Division title, the European Cup and the UEFA Super Cup

Clue3: My only Villa goal was in a 3-2 home win over Norwich City

Clue4: I made 4 appearances for the Republic of Ireland

Clue5: I was born in Galway where I played football before and after my Villa career

Who Am I - Player 12

Clue1: I played for 11 English clubs but the club I made most career appearances for was Stoke City

Clue2: I played in two different World Cup tournaments

Clue3: The club I left to join Villa and the club I left Villa for are local rivals

Clue4: I have written two football based books and also feature in a series of podcasts

Clue5: I celebrated some goals with a 'Robot Dance'

Who Am I - Player 13

Clue1: I have a League Cup winners medal with Villa, but was later transferred away from Villa Park by Brian Little

Clue2: My next team won the FA Cup, but I was cup-tied

Clue3: I had spells, in the late nineties, playing for both Sheffield clubs

Clue4: I was given three England Caps by Graham Taylor

Clue5: My first cap was while playing for Oldham Athletic, the club I made most appearances for in my career.

Who Am I - Player 14

Clue1: After Villa, I played for Everton

Clue2: I have been named PFA Player's Player of the Year

Clue3: I helped Villa win the UEFA Intertoto Cup

Clue4: I appeared on I'm a Celebrity Get me Out of Here

Clue5: I won 17 caps for France

Who Am I - Player 15

Clue1: I was signed by Ron Atkinson for Villa

Clue2: I scored 12 goals in nearly a decade at Villa Park

Clue3: I had a spell with Glasgow Rangers

Clue4: I scored my only senior England goal at Villa Park

Clue5: I played for Sheffield United while Lee Hendrie was also with the Blades

Who Am I - Player 16

Clue1: While having several clubs abroad, apart from Villa, I have only played for one other club in England where I scored 19 goals in 49 games

Clue2: I was born in France

Clue3: I have played in the Africa Cup of Nations

Clue4: My first Villa goal was against Brentford

Clue5: My on field injury began the series of events that led to the controversial goal scored by Leeds in April 2019

Who Am I - Player 17

Clue1: I scored a winning goal in a World Cup match
Clue2: I made over 120 appearances for Fulham
Clue3: I played in Villa's first ever Premier League match
Clue4: I won a League Cup medal twice, once with Villa and once with Oxford United
Clue5: I joined Villa from Liverpool

Who Am I - Player 18

Clue1: I am a centre back
Clue2: I made more appearances for Walsall than I did Villa
Clue3: I have won the League title, FA Cup and UEFA Cup Winner's Cup
Clue4: I was signed for Villa by Graham Taylor
Clue5: I won all my major honours with Everton

Who Am I - Player 19

Clue1: I was a Martin O'Neill signing for Villa, having played for him before
Clue2: I also played for another ex-Villa manager later in my career at a club in the North of England
Clue3: I have an FA Cup winners medal
Clue4: I had a spell with the coaching staff of the Belgian International team
Clue5: In 2023 I began managing the club I won the FA Cup with

Who Am I - Player 20

Clue1: I once had a spell on loan at Nottingham Forest

Clue2: My only goal for Villa was scored against Fulham

Clue3: I have been on the coaching staff at Leicester City

Clue4: I have winners medals in all domestic competitions, UEFA Champions League and Europa League with the same club

Clue5: I spent 19 years as a senior player for Chelsea

Map Quiz 3 – England Villans

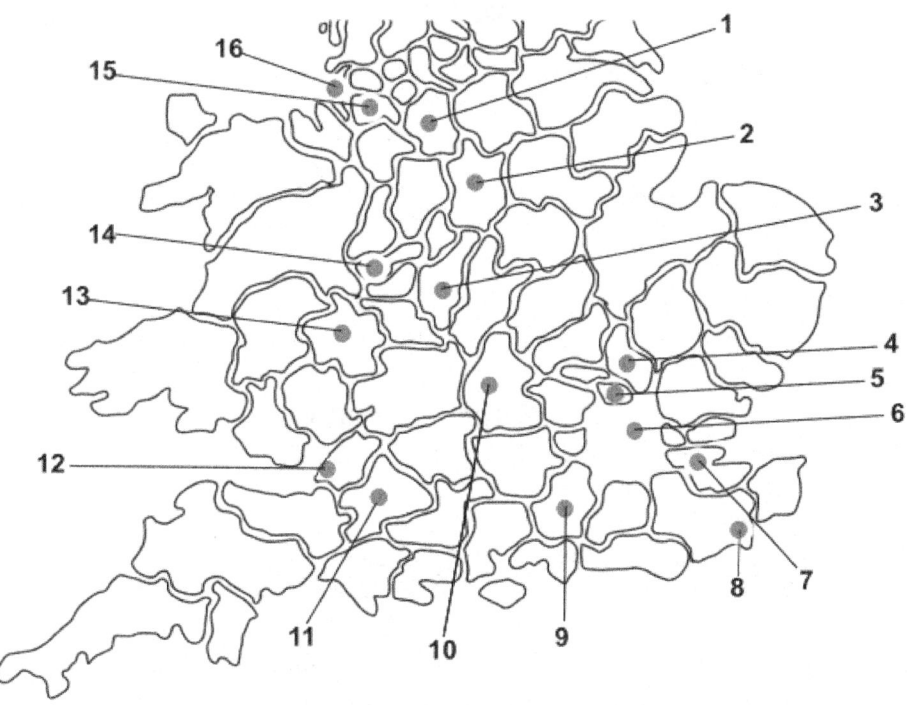

This is a map of postcode areas with sixteen labelled. Each postcode area contains the city or town that is birthplace of a player from the list below. Can you match each player with the correct location?

Gareth Barry, Frank Carrodus, Ugo Ehiogu, John Gidman
Tony Hateley, David James, Martin Keown, Tyrone Mings
Chris Nicholl, Chris Price, Bruce Rioch, John Sleeuwenhoek
Andy Townsend, Darius Vassell, Ray Graydon, Ashley Young

5 Aside: Former Favourites

5 Aside: Stiliyan Petrov

1 Which country did Stiliyan represent internationally, winning over 100 caps?
2 Martin O'Neill signed him for Villa, from which club?
3 In which season did he win Villa's Player of the Year and Player's Player of the Year Awards?
4 What shirt number did he wear for most of his career at Villa?
5 Who did he succeed as club captain at Villa?

5 Aside: Alan Hutton

1 Which manager signed Alan for Villa?
2 As he made more appearances, Alan became more appreciated by the supporters. What nickname did he become known by?
3 Alan Hutton was not picked for the first team for two consecutive seasons under which Villa manager?
4 Originally given the squad number of 2, this number changed when he returned to regular first team action and remained until his retirement. What was it?
5 How many full caps did Alan win for Scotland? A: 20, B: 30 C: 40 D: 50

5 Aside: Gabriel Agbonlahor

1 In what area of Birmingham was Gabby born?
2 Which Yorkshire club did he have a loan spell with in 2005?
3 Which team did he make his first team Villa appearance against?
4 How many league and cup goals did he score for Villa against Birmingham City?
5 Gabby made 3 appearances for England. Can you name any of the opponent countries he faced?

5 Aside: Charlie Aitken

1 Charlie is Villa's all time leading appearance-maker. How many did he make in all competitions?
2 What is the title of his semi-autobiography?
3 Charlie had his best scoring season in the 3rd Division Championship season. What link was there between the 4 goals he scored?
4 Charlie's Villa career ended under the management of Ron Saunders. How many other different managers did he play for while with Aston Villa?
5 After Villa he played in the United States. For which team?

5 Aside: Jhon Durán

1 Which MLS team did he leave to join Villa?
2 Which country does he represent at international level?
3 Which club did he join after leaving Villa?
4 His first two Premier League goals were both from substitute appearances against Everton and Crystal Palace. Which goal was scored closest to the end of 90 minutes?
5 Which midlands team did he make his Villa debut against?

5 Aside: Juan Pablo Ángel

1 Which manager let Ángel go to New York Red Bulls on a free transfer?
2 Which country did he play international football for?
3 The most goals he scored in total against any club in Premier League matches is 4. This happened with 4 different opponents. However he also had the record of never being on the losing side against only one of them. Which club is this? A: Bolton Wanderers, B: Blackburn Rovers, C: Fulham, D: Wolverhampton Wanderers
4 Which club was he signed from when he joined Villa?
5 His last Villa goal came in December 2006 in a 2-2 draw away to which opponents?

5 Aside: Alan McInally

1 Which club did Alan join Villa from?
2 Which movie character did he share a nickname with?
3 He made one appearance for Scotland at the 1990 World Cup. Against which country?
4 Which Scottish team did he finish his playing career with?
5 His debut goal for Villa came in a home League Cup match where 2nd division Villa beat a club in the top flight 2-1. Who did they win against?

5 Aside: Albert Adomah

1 Which manager signed Albert Adomah for Villa?
2 True or False? Villa never lost a game where Albert Adomah scored.
3 What was Albert's shirt number?
4 Which country has he been capped for?
5 Which club did he join after leaving Villa?

140

5 Aside: Allan Evans

1 How many appearances did Allan make for Villa? A: 342, B: 412, C: 472, D: 502

2 True/False Allan was the last of the 1st Division title winning squad to leave the club?

3 Allan Evans twice had a best season goals tally of 10. The first was in 1979/80. Which was the other, helped by the fact most came from the penalty spot?

4 In their Championship Title winning year, Villa won every game that Allan scored in, bar one. Which team won that game 1-2?

5 Which club was Allan Evans signed from when he joined Villa?

5 Aside: Ashley Young

1 Ashley wore the number 7 for the majority of his first stint as a Villa player, however he wore a different number in his very first season. What was it?

2 Where did he join Villa from in his second stint, this time under Dean Smith?

3 Ashley Young only made it into one of England's World Cup squads. Was it A: 2010, B: 2014, C: 2018, D: 2022?

4 In which season with Villa did he win the PFA Young Player of the Year Award?

5 He went to the same school and was in the same year group as which World Champion sportsman?

5 Aside: Brian Little

1 Brian's best season for goals in league and cups saw a tally of 26. Which season was it?

2 Villa only lost a total of eight games in which Brian Little scored. Only one team appears twice in that list. Is it? A: Fulham, B: Liverpool, C: Newcastle United, D: Nottingham Forest

3 In 2014, Brian became Director of Football at which British Crown Dependency?

4 Which Welsh team did he have a spell managing?

5 Brian Little played his first senior game for Villa in European competition against which team?

5 Aside: Christian Benteke

1 Christian Benteke made 101 appearances for Villa. How many goals did he score? A: 34, B: 39, C: 44, D: 49

2 After Villa, Benteke had spells with Liverpool and Crystal Palace before moving on to the USA to play for which MLS team?

3 Which was Benteke's last game as a Villa player?

4 How many hat-tricks did he score for Villa?

5 What was his Villa shirt number?

5 Aside: Dalian Atkinson

1 Which Turkish club did Dalian join after leaving Villa?
2 Dalian made an excellent start to the Premier League where he scored in each of the first 3 matches. These also ended in the same score, what was it?
3 During the First Division and Premier League with Villa, his largest total goals tally against any club was 4. Who did he score these goals against over three different matches?
4 Which club did he begin his senior football career with?
5 Who was the goalkeeper he beat with his wonder goal, celebrated under an umbrella?

5 Aside: Darius Vassell

1 Which manager handed Darius his Villa debut?
2 Which World Cup tournament was he a part of England's squad?
3 True or False? Villa never lost a League game where Darius Vassell scored.
4 Which club did he join after a brief spell playing in Turkey?
5 Vassell scored an impressive bicycle kick on his England debut. Who were the opposition?

5 Aside: David Platt

1 Which club did he leave to sign for Villa?
2 Platt's final goal of Villa's 1987/88 promotion season was the winner in a crucial 1-0 home defeat of which promotion rivals?
3 Which Italian club did he leave Villa for?
4 David scored his first 3 international goals against 3 different countries at the 1990 World Cup. Which match saw his first?
5 Who did he score 4 goals against in a 1993 qualifying game for the 1994 World Cup?

5 Aside: Dion Dublin

1 Dion Dublin's last Villa goal came in a 5-0 rout at which Midlands rivals?
2 Dion Dublin was the first ever scorer in a Wembley play-off final. Who was he playing for?
3 Dion ended his league career back at the club he started as a youth. Which team?
4 Which future Villa keeper was on the receiving end of a bizarre goal in 1997 when he placed the ball unaware that Dion Dublin, playing for Coventry City, was right behind him?
5 Who did he have a brief loan spell for while still very much a Villa player?

5 Aside: Dwight Yorke

1 Who did Dwight Yorke play international football for?

2 How many different Villa managers did he play under?

3 Which club did he finish his playing career with?

4 Yorke only played league football for one team outside of England. Who were they?

5 Who did Dwight score more goals for. Villa or Manchester United?

5 Aside: Tony Daley

1 How old was Tony when he made his first team Villa debut?

2 After leaving Villa, Tony played for three clubs that all begin with the same letter. Can you name them?

3 Which major tournament saw Tony make appearances for England?

4 Who was the last Villa manager Tony Daley played under?

5 After retiring, Tony Daley had a spell as fitness coach with which club until he reportedly fell out with their manager, Bryan Robson?

5 Aside: Nathan Delfouneso

1 What was Nathan's nickname among the Villa supporters?
2 While with Villa, he went out on loan several times including to Blackpool where he would eventually become a permanent member of the club. Can you name any of the others he was loaned to?
3 Nathan made his Villa debut in a UEFA cup match under Martin O'Neill. How old was he?
4 Delfouneso scored two league goals for Villa, his first was against Portsmouth, who was the second against?
5 As recently as October 2023, Nathan turned out for which National League North team in a Lancashire Cup tie?

5 Aside: Mark Draper

1 Throughout his Villa career, Draper kept the same squad number. What was it?
2 Mark Draper made over 200 appearances for his first club. Who are they?
3 Who did Mark Draper score his first Villa goal against?
4 Which club did he sign for after leaving Villa?
5 Which England manager picked Mark Draper for his England main squad? (He had been selected for England training squads before this).

5 Aside: Jack Grealish

1 Although he made one appearance for Villa, Jack spent much of the 2013-14 season on loan to which club?
2 While with Villa, Jack had 3 different squad numbers. What were they?
3 Which manager made him the regular Villa captain?
4 Which country did he make his senior England debut against?
5 In the 2015/16 relegation season, Jack played in 16 Premier League games. How many points out of 42 did Villa accrue in these? A: 0, B: 3, C: 6 D: 9

5 Aside: Lee Hendrie

1 How many appearances did Lee Hendrie make for Villa? A: 150+, B: 200+, C: 250+, D: 300+
2 Lee Hendrie won one full England cap against which European opposition?
3 Like Jack Grealish, Lee also had 3 different squad numbers at Villa. What were they?
4 Lee scored his first Premier League goal for Villa against which local rivals?
5 Lee has turned out for several non-league sides. Which one has he made the most appearances for?

5 Aside: Conor Hourihane

1 From which club did Villa sign Conor?

2 Who were the last opponents Conor scored against in open play in the 2018-19 promotion season?

3 Which country has he represented at international level?

4 Conor had two loan spells while on Villa's books, one was with Sheffield United, who was the other?

5 While with Villa in the Championship, Hourihane scored against the same club in three different matches at Villa Park. Overall the final scores totalled 9-1 in Villa's favour. Who were the opponents?

5 Aside: Julian Joachim

1 Which manager signed Julian for Villa?

2 Julian scored for Villa once in European competition. Who were the opposition who Villa beat on their own turf in 1998?

3 After a spell with Leeds and a loan at Walsall, Julian played for two League 2 clubs. Both would later be relegated to non-league. Who were they?

4 Julian had a very good scoring record in his 6 seasons at Villa, scoring 44 goals. His best season at Villa was the 1998/99 season. How many did he score in all competitions? A: 10, B: 12, C: 14 D: 16

5 After being handed the number 26 shirt in his first season, which number did he wear for the rest of his Villa career?

5 Aside: Martin Laursen

1 From which team did Villa sign Martin Laursen?

2 Martin Laursen played in all of Denmark's games at the 2002 World Cup. Which team knocked them out?

3 After retiring, Martin made a farewell appearance pre-match at Villa Park when they hosted which team?

4 Before joining Villa, Laursen won the Champions League with the club from question 1. Who did they beat in the final?

5 Martin scored twelve goals in his Villa career. Although not in a single game, he got 25% of these against which club?

5 Aside: Paul McGrath

1 Despite not joining Villa until he was 29. Paul McGrath made a lot of appearances for Villa. Was his total? A: 200+, B: 250+, C: 300+, D: 350+

2 True or False? Villa never lost a game where Paul McGrath scored.

3 Which manager signed Paul McGrath for Villa?

4 In which season, did he win the PFA Player's Player of the Year Award?

5 Which club did he join after leaving Villa?

5 Aside: James Milner

1 What number did Milner wear when on loan to Villa. (It was not No.8)?

2 Villa never lost a league match when Milner scored. Of his 22 goals, how many came in cup matches? A: 0, B: 4, C: 10, D:14

3 Despite winning over 60 international caps, James Milner has only scored one goal for England. It came in a 5-0 victory over which country's team?

4 James Milner won the Villa Goal of the Season award in 2009/10 for a 25 yard thunderbolt. Who were the opponents?

5 To date, he has only played for one team outside the Premier League. Who was the club?

149

5 Aside: Savo Milošević

1 Which item of clothing was he solely responsible for it being on sale in the club shop?
2 Savo scored one hat-trick for Villa. This was in a 4-1 win over which team?
3 Which Spanish club did he sign for after leaving Villa?
4 Savo was joint top goalscorer at Euro 2000. How many did he score?
5 In 2023, Savo was appointed head coach for which national team?

5 Aside: Kevin Richardson

1 Ron Atkinson signed Kevin, from which Spanish club?
2 Which city was Kevin's birthplace? A: Newcastle-On-Tyne, B: Liverpool C: London D: Manchester
3 Kevin Richardson won his only England cap while he was Aston Villa captain. Who were the opponents in a friendly? A: Belgium, B: Greece, C: Iceland, D: Portugal
4 Who signed Richardson for Coventry City from Villa?
5 Kevin Richardson won the First Division title with two different teams. Who were they?

5 Aside: Dean Saunders

1 Dean Saunders began his career with two Welsh clubs, one his parent club, the other in a loan spell. Which were they?
2 Saunders scored one hat-trick among his 50 goals for Villa. This came in a 5-0 home win in the 1993/94 season over which team?
3 Dean Saunders had a particular liking for scoring against the same club in four separate fixtures while with Villa. Was it? A: Ipswich Town, B: Liverpool, C: Sheffield Wednesday, D: Wimbledon

4 Which club was he playing for when he scored a cheeky goal by taking a quick throw in against the back of a hastily retreating goalkeeper before shooting into an empty net? Clue: The goalkeeper was playing for Port Vale.
5 Which Turkish club did he sign for on leaving Villa? A: Beşiktaş, B: Fenerbahçe, C: Galatasaray, D: Trabzonspor

5 Aside: Gareth Southgate

1 True or False. Although Gareth made more than 240 appearances for Villa, he was never named as a substitute?
2 Gareth Southgate scored 9 goals for Villa and Villa won every game he scored in. Three of his Villa goals were against one of these Yorkshire clubs. Was it A: Barnsley, B: Bradford City, C: Leeds, D: Sheffield Wednesday?
3 Southgate only played for two other league teams. Who were they?
4 Gareth was only sent off once and it was while playing for Villa. He also scored an own goal in that same game. Who were the opponents?
5 After Euro 96, Southgate appeared in a TV advert with Stuart Pearce and Chris Waddle. Which company was it for?

5 Aside: Nigel Spink

1 How many seasons did Nigel spend with Villa? A:11, B: 13, C: 15, D: 17
2 Nigel's England career occurred while a Villa player. It lasted 45 minutes after he was a substitute in a friendly against which non-European team?
3 Spink had a spell as goalkeeper coach with Bristol City and he also had a similar role at three other clubs working for Steve Bruce. Not including Birmingham City, can you name either of the other two?
4 Nigel played for three teams after leaving Villa. Which one did he make the most appearances for?
5 Nigel Spink saved 3 penalties while with Villa. Oddly, the outcome of each match was a draw and further, 2 were against Liverpool in different games. Which 2 players did he deny from their spot-kicks?

5 Aside: Ian Taylor

1 Ian Taylor played in three matches for Villa where he scored more than one goal. The first instance was an away win at Coventry City and the last at home to Spurs. The second was in a League Cup tie that went to extra time. This was away to which club?

2 Which manager sold Ian to Derby County?

3 Ian Taylor scored many times. But he had a knack of scoring against one particular club the most, finding the net in 4 different fixtures. Which team was this?

4 Ian's current links with Villa are well known, he has been appointed a member of the Honorary Anniversary Board ahead of Villa's 150th anniversary season, and has a regular feature in the News and Record. What is this called?

5 Which legend of the Potteries gave Ian Taylor his league career debut at Port Vale?

5 Aside: Gareth Barry

1 Although he scored over 50 goals for Villa, Gareth only scored two goals in second half added on time. One was a consolation goal against Birmingham City, while the other was an equaliser in a game full of incident. Who were the opponents?

2 How many senior matches did he play for Villa? A: 400, B: 440 C: 480, D: 520

3 Which manager handed him his senior England debut?

4 Gareth was sent off 3 times in his Villa career. He received two straight reds against Portsmouth and Charlton and two yellows away to which London club?

5 Gareth Barry had 3 different squad numbers while playing for Villa. He is best known for wearing number 6, but what were the other two?

5 Aside: Paul Merson

1 True or False. Merson joined Villa from Arsenal?
2 At which World Cup Finals did he play for England?
3 What was odd about his debut Villa goal which came at home to Wimbledon?
4 With which midlands club did he have a spell as Player/Manager?
5 His best goals per game ratio came with the club he signed for after Villa. Who were they?

5 Aside: Ian 'Chico' Hamilton

1 Tommy Docherty signed Chico for Aston Villa having worked with him previously at which club?
2 Which club were paid £40,000 to bring Chico to Villa Park
3 True of False: While at the Villa, Chico had boutique store in Wylde Green?
4 When Chico was transferred from Villa he joined a 2nd Division team and after them he joined which North American Soccer team?
5 After his playing career, Chico worked as a 'Football in the Community Officer' in which English county?

5 Aside: – Ron Saunders

1 How many seasons did Ron Saunders lead a team out at Wembley for a League Cup Final? between 1973 and 1977
2 True or False: Ron Saunders began his playing career as a Right Back?
3 Before long at Villa, Ron Saunders' programme notes ended with the same statement about being confident we can get the right result. What percentage contribution did he demand from the players?
4 Who was Birmingham City chairman when Ron joined them as manager?
5 Ron was invited to Villa Park twice and accepted both during the 2006-07 season. Can you name either of the teams who were Villa's opponents?

5 Aside: Ian Ross

1 Which legendary manager signed Ian Ross for Liverpool towards the beginning of his football career?
2 Who did Ian Ross succeed as Villa captain?
3 In the promotion season of 74/75, Ian Ross became the last senior outfield player on the team to score a goal. Who did he get his first goal of that campaign against?
4 In the 1980's, Ian Ross had a six month spell managing a European team who Villa had met in a European Cup campaign. Can you name the club?
5 Towards the end of his Villa career, Ian Ross had two short loans. One was with Notts County, who was the other one with?

5 Aside: – James 'Jimmy ' Cumbes

1 Jimmy joined Villa from West Bromwich Albion. Which team did he play for immediately before them?
2 Who was the West Brom manager who limited Cumbes' first team appearances preferring John Osborne?
3 True of False: While at the Villa, Jimmy had a radio show on Radio Birmingham?
4 What did Jimmy Cumbes have in common with fellow players Chris Balderstone and Ted Hemsley?
5 After Villa, Jimmy had a season playing in North America for which team?

5 Aside: Douglas Luiz

1 Although on Manchester City's books, Douglas never played a senior match for them. Instead he was loaned out to which Spanish affiliate team?
2 Douglas Luiz scored directly from a Villa corner in a Premier League match. Who did he score against?

154

3 In 2002, he had a red card rescinded following a clash with which then Fulham player?

4 In 2024, Luiz joined which Italian Serie A club?

5 As well as winning a medal at the delayed 2020 Olympics, Douglas was also a member of the Brazil squad that finished runners up in the 2021 Copa América. Which team beat them 1-0 in the final?

And Finally: Villa in Print

Can you match these Autobiographical or Biographical Titles with the correct players and/or managers listed?

1 From Mine to Milan
2 Back from the Brink
3 Here, There and Everywhere
4 The Manager
5 On Days Like These
6 All for the Love of the Game
7 One
8 Ask a Footballer
9 In His Own Words
10 Hooked
11 Deadly!
12 The Road to Persia
13 Going for Goal
14 Hail Cesar
15 The Curse of Pele
16 Born to Score
17 The Odd Man Out
18 Football With a Smile
19 The Boss
20 Achieving the Goal

Billy McNeill, Darius Vassell, David Platt, Dwight Yorke, Gerry Hitchens, Graham Taylor, James Milner, Joe Mercer, John Gregory, Martin O'Neill, Nii Lamptey, Paul McGrath, Paul Merson, Peter McParland, Peter Schmeicel, Peter Withe, Shaun Teale, Ron Atkinson, Ron Saunders, Sir Doug Ellis

ANSWERS

Answers – Question Set One – Champions League Season

1 Emi Martinez
2 Diego Carlos
3 Amadou Onana
4 Lamare Bogarde
5 Ollie Watkins
6 Watkins and Durán
7 Portman Road, Ipswich
8 Wycombe Wanderers
9 Chris Heck
10 Pau Torres
11 Pau Torres
12 A
13 C
14 C
15 Morgan Rogers
16 Matty Cash
17 Jaden Philogene
18 Samuel Iling-Junior
19 John McGinn
20 Chris Kavanagh
21 D
22 German
23 Anfield, Liverpool
24 Youri Tielemans
25 Ross Barkley
26 Morgan Rogers
27 Matty Cash
28 Red Bull Arena
29 John McGinn

30 Leipzig 2 Aston Villa 3

31 Youri Tielemans

32 Anthony Taylor

33 Wham! Last Christmas

34 Leon Bailey

35 Jamaldeen Jimoh-Aloba

36 Black

37 1996/97

38 Idrissa Gueye and Ashley Young

39 Lucas Digne

40 A

41 Donyell Malen

42 Ozzy Osbourne

43 Hibs, Rangers and Queens Park

44 Liverpool, Barcelona, Arsenal, Inter Milan, Atlético, Leverkusen & Lille

45 Gary Shaw, Peter Withe, Stan Collymore and Ollie Watkins

46 Onana, Malen, Maatsen and Bailey

47 Tottenham Hotspur

48 Axel Tuanzebe

49 Andrés Garcia

50 Arne Slot

51 Marco Asensio

52 Ian Maatsen & Lamar Bogarde

53 Tyrone Mings

54 A

55 B

56 Gordon Cowans and Dennis Mortimer

57 Dion Dublin

58 Ezri Konsa, Marcus Rashford and Morgan Rogers (as a substitute)

59 Manchester United

60 Six

61 Donyell Malen

62 B

63 Garcia, Disasi, Mings, Maaatsen, Onana, Malen, Asensio, Watkins

64 C

65 Youri Tielemans

66 Sam Proctor

67 Matty Cash

68 Left

69 Three! Watkins, Malen and McGinn

70 £1.50 (150 years celebrations), £3 (Carabao Cup), £4 (Regular Season) and £5 (Champions League)

71 This is Villa Park

72 The Europa League theme

73 Marcus Rashford

74 Ross Barkley

75 B

76 Ian Maatsen

77 Amadou Onana

78 Samuel Illing-Junior

79 Jacob Ramsey

80 John McGinn

81 75

82 Boubacar Kamara

83 Youri Tielemans

84 PSG

85 Manchester City

86 Thomas Bramall

87 Morgan Rogers

88 Malmo

89 Ezri Konsa

90 RB Leipzig

Answers – 5 Aside: The Current Squad

Answers - 5 Aside: Emilio Martinez

1 Oxford United, Sheffield Wednesday, Wolverhampton Wanderers, Rotherham United and Reading
2 2019-2020
3 John Lundstram, Sheffield United
4 C: 34
5 Two (Argentina won 4-2)

Answers - 5 Aside: John McGinn

1 St Mirren
2 Paul
3 Tottenham Hotspur
4 Southampton
5 'The Goggles'

Answers - 5 Aside: Evann Guessand

1 Nice
2 Ivory Coast
3 29
4 Emi Buendia
5 Crystal Palace

Answers - 5 Aside: Jaden Sancho

1 True, for Borussia Dortmund
2 Manchester United

161

3 St Mary's Southampton
4 D: 23
5 It was saved

Answers - 5 Aside: Harvey Elliott

1 PSG
2 Blackburn Rovers
3 Fulham
4 Germany
5 9-0

Answers - 5 Aside: Matty Cash

1 Nottingham Forest
2 Burnley
3 Poland
4 Dagenham and Redbridge
5 Hibernian and Lille

Answers - 5 Aside: Tyrone Mings

1 40
2 Ipswich Town
3 Reading
4 San Marino
5 Rotherham and Crystal Palace

Answers - 5 Aside: Donyell Malen

1 The Netherlands
2 Arsenal
3 Nottingham Forest
4 17

5 Borussia Dortmund

Answers - 5 Aside: Ezri Konsa

1 Charlton Athletic
2 Crewe Alexandra
3 North Macedonia
4 Watford
5 14

Answers - 5 Aside: Youri Tielemans

1 Anderlecht
2 Sheffield United
3 Chelsea
4 Romania
5 Leon Bailey

Answers - 5 Aside: Ollie Watkins

1 Exeter City
2 Brighton and Hove Albion
3 Under Armour
4 The Netherlands
5 Five

Answers - 5 Aside: Lucas Digne

1 Rafa Benitez
2 Manchester United
3 PSG and Barcelona
4 Idrissa Gueye
5 Brazil 2014

Answers - 5 Aside: Pau Torres

1 Spurs
2 14
3 Villarreal
4 Manchester United
5 Silver

Answers -5 Aside: Ian Maatsen

1 The Netherlands
2 Charlton Athletic or Coventry City
3 Borussia Dortmund
4 Athletico Madrid
5 Burnley

Answers - 5 Aside: Ross Barkley

1 Leeds United or Sheffield Wednesday
2 True
3 Chelsea
4 Nice
5 Five

Answers - 5 Aside: Marco Bizot

1 Brest
2 The Netherlands
3 Newcastle United
4 AZ Alkmaar
5 6' 4" (1.94m)

Answers - 5 Aside: Victor Lindelof

1 Sweden
2 Russia 2018
3 Jose Mourinho
4 Benfica
5 False, he was a free transfer

Answers - 5 Aside: Emi Buendia

1 Norwich
2 Bayer Leverkusen
3 True, against Colombia
4 Brentford
5 Dean Smith

Answers - 5 Aside: Boubacar Kamara

1 Everton
2 Brentford
3 Olympique Marseille
4 Senegal
5 44

Answers - 5 Aside: Morgan Rogers

1 Middlesborough
2 Brentford
3 27
4 Bournemouth or Blackpool
5 Lincoln City

Answers - 5 Aside: Unai Emery

1 October
2 Real Sociedad
3 Almeria
4 Arsene Wenger
5 Sevilla

Answers – Map Quiz 1 – African Villans

Player	No	Player	No	Player	No
Jonathan Kodjia	5	Rudy Gestede	8	Yacouba Sylla	9
Mbwana Samatta	15	Albert Adomah	6	Moustapha Salifou	7
Curtis Davies	4	Habib Beye	3	Trezeguet	1
Bernard Traore	10	Yannick Bolasie	13	Hassan Kachloul	2
Marvelous Nakamba	14	Eric Djemba-Djemba	11	Christopher Samba	12

Answers – Villanagrams 1

1 Ken Swain

2 Dennis Mortimer

3 Peter Withe

4 Nigel Spink

5 Ollie Watkins

6 Pau Torres

7 Jack Grealish

8 Guy Whittingham

9 Ian Maatsen

10 Stan Collymore

11 Martin Laursen

12 Tommy Docherty

13 Phil Woosnam

14 Charlie Aitken

15 Willie Anderson

16 Ashley Young

17 Tyrone Mings

18 Dean Saunders

19 Jimmy Hogan

20 Christian Benteke

166

Answers – Starting XI – Quiz 1

Martinez

Konsa Torres Carlos Digne

Onana Tielemens Ramsey Philogene

Rogers Watkins

Answers – Tenable – Quiz 1

1. Glasgow Celtic (42,834)
2. Nottingham Forest (42,743)
3. Manchester United (42,682)
4. Newcastle United (42,618)
5. Juventus (42,589)
6. Paris Saint-Germain (42,535)
7. Fulham (42,515)
8. Ipswich Town (42,510)
9. Club Brugge (42,461)
10. Southampton (42,453)

Answers - Beginnings I - The 19th Century

1 The FA Cup
2 A: Play as goalkeeper
3 Old Crown and Cushion
4 Stoke City
5 2nd
6 Accrington Stanley
7 Rampant
8 William McGregor
9 Ready
10 Newtown Row
11 A: Canadian
12 C: 1906
13 A: £250
14 Glasgow Rangers
15 Crewe
16 Kennington Oval
17 Sports Argus
18 1897
19 He scored the first ever goal at Villa Park
20 Summer Lane

Answers - Beginnings II - A New Century

1 Queen Victoria died
2 Harry Hampton
3 The Midland Bank
4 A cycle track

5 True

6 He is the only player to win 3 FA Cup winner's medals while representing Villa.

7 The Final was scheduled for Stamford Bridge which would not have been neutral had Chelsea won

8 Liverpool

9 Billy Kirton

10 Villa wanted all players to be living locally

11 Billy Walker

12 Tommy Ball

13 The final was made all-ticket for the first time.

14 70,000

15 Joe Bache

16 It was a Central League match! (Villa reserves versus Birmingham City reserves)

17 20 games

18 49, he also scored one goal in the FA Cup

19 Eric Houghton

20 Rhyl

21 Wales

22 1936

23 Middlesbrough, West Bromwich Albion, Arsenal

24 They were the last of the original members of the Football League to lose their top tier status

25 D: 81

26 James Hogan

27 C: Swansea Town

28 Preston North End

29 Frank Broome

30 It was the first time they had worn numbers on their shirts in a league game.

Answers - Post-WWII Forties And Fifties

1 The tie was a two-legged affair, Villa won 3-2 on aggregate?

2 Four

3 D: It was a 35 yard header

4 Walsall

5 Five

6 Peter McParland

7 Johnny Dixon

8 Derek 'Doc' Pace

9 Peter McParland

10 The match was to mark the official opening of Villa's new floodlights

11 Joe Mercer

12 Trevor Ford

13 Notts County

14 Thomson

15 Stan Lynn

16 Charlton Athletic

17 Five

18 Bristol City

19 Semi-Final

20 Bobby Thomson

Answers – Villanagrams 2

1 Ashley Westwood

2 Tim Sherwood

3 Morgan Rogers

4 Steve McMahon

5 Stewart Downing

6 Gareth Southgate

7 Hassan Kachloul

8 George Boateng

9 Pat McMahon

10 Paul Merson

11 Leandro Bacuna

12 Eric Houghton

13 Savo Milosevic

14 Gabriel Agbonlahor

15 George Curtis

16 Mark Delaney

17 Stiliyan Petrov

18 Graham Taylor

19 Lee Hendrie

20 Gary Shelton

Answers – Starting XI – Quiz 2

James

Delaney Staunton Southgate Wright

Boateng Barry Taylor Merson

Dublin Vassell

Answers – Tenable – Quiz 2

1. Arsenal
2. Everton (twice)
3. Newcastle United (twice)
4. Sheffield United (closed doors)
5. Bournemouth
6. Wigan Athletic
7. Hull City
8. Rotherham United
9. Manchester United
10. Liverpool

Answers – Question set 3 – The Fortune Swinging Sixties

Answers -The Warm Up

1 1962
2 Tony Hateley
3 Most were letters, spelling ASTON VILLA
4 Mansfield Town
5 Geoff Vowden (for Birmingham City)
6 Birmingham City
7 Colin Withers
8 Tommy Docherty
9 Luton Town
10 A: Portugal

Answers -Before the 1966 World Cup

1 Huddersfield Town
2 Villa 6-2 Birmingham City

172

3 Tottenham Hotspur

4 Russia

5 Charlie Aitken

6 Rotherham United

7 Derek Dougan

8 Arsenal

9 C: 8-3

10 Harry Burrows

11 West Ham United and Wales

12 Fog

13 D: March 7th

14 11

15 A nil-nil draw, meaning Villa lost 1-3 on aggregate.

16 Denis Law

17 Aldershot Town

18 Birmingham City

19 Nigel Sims

20 Chelsea

21 Tony Hateley

22 Sunderland

23 Chelsea

24 Colin Withers

25 Stoke City

26 Northampton Town

27 He was Villa's first ever used substitute

28 West Ham United

29 Tottenham Hotspur 5-5 Aston Villa

30 Twente Enschede

Answers -After the 1966 World Cup

1 Derek Dougan

2 Lew Chatterley

3 D: 31,570 (The 3rd highest attendance at Villa Park that season!)

4 John Sleeuwenhoek

5 Everton

6 Wilson Briggs

7 Rotherham United, Millwall and Carlisle United

8 Brian Godfrey

9 Harry Gregory

10 Queens Park Rangers

11 Tottenham Hotspur

12 Mr Norman Smith

13 Norwich City

14 Brian Tiler

15 Jimmy Brown

Answers – Starting XI – Quiz 3

Martinez

Cash Konsa Mings Targett

Luiz McGinn Barkley Trezeguet

Grealish Watkins

Answers – Tenable – Quiz 3

1. Adidas
2. Castore
3. Kappa
4. Luke 1977
5. Under Armour
6. Macron
7. Nike
8. Hummel
9. Diadora
10. Reebok

Answers – Question Set 4 – From Rotherham to Rotterdam

Answers - The Warm-Up

1 Vic Crowe
2 Santos
3 Jimmy Cumbes
4 D: 48,110
5 Willie Anderson
6 Ron Wylie
7 Preston North End
8 Bodymoor Heath
9 Brighton and Hove Albion
10 Tottenham Hotspur

Answers - 1970-71 A First Time for Everything

1 It was 3:15 rather than 3:00
2 Green
3 Lionel Martin
4 Charlton Athletic
5 Reading
6 Pat McMahon
7 Two, it was 23rd December
8 Geoff Crudgington
9 Steve Perryman
10 Martin Chivers

Answers - 1971-72 The Long Road Back

1 Villa 2 Birmingham City 1

2 Pat McMahon

3 The Hawthorns

4 Bristol Rovers

5 Mansfield Town

6 A 4-4 draw

7 Torquay United (70) and Southend United (71)

8 Tommy Hughes

9 It remained 4-1 at full time

10 Andy Lochhead

11 Charlie Aitken

12 It had four players with their backs to the camera with the shirt numbers 1, 9, 7 and 2

13 Jim Cumbes

14 Green and Black Stripes

15 Luton Town

16 Wrexham (A), Swansea City (H) and Bristol Rovers (H)

17 Ray Graydon

18 George Curtis

19 Brian Little

20 Chesterfield

21 70

22 B: Ray Graydon

23 Walsall

24 Liverpool

25 None, they lost every match!

Answers - 1972-73 Upward Momentum

1 Francis Lee
2 On their sleeves
3 Huddersfield Town
4 Hereford United
5 John Gidman
6 Derby County
7 Burnley
8 Cardiff City
9 Ray Graydon
10 Brian Tiler
11 Oldham Athletic
12 The top 3 being promoted rule came in a season later

Answers - 1973-74 99 Not Out

1 Sir Bobby Charlton
2 Norwich City
3 Bruce Rioch
4 Jimmy Sirrell
5 Tony 'Bomber' Brown
6 Sammy Morgan
7 Villa 2 Arsenal 0
8 Derby County
9 Keith Leonard
10 They were played 24 hours apart over the Easter break (Home on 15th April, Away on 16th April)
11 Jake Findlay
12 B: Feyenoord,

Answers - 1974-75   A Very Special Centenary

1 Brian Clough

2 Everton

3 A: £10

4 Manchester City

5 York City

6 Villa 6 Hull City 0

7 Derby County

8 Everton

9 A: Ray Graydon

10 D: A firework

11 Colchester United

12 Chester City

13 Frank Pimblett

14 Sheffield United

15 A huge bottle of Bell's Whiskey

16 Charlie Aitken

17 B: £2.50

18 Mel Machin

19 Kevin Keelan

20 The goalkeeper's right

21 Ronald Bendall

22 Sam Allardyce

23 We're Going Up!

24 A helicopter hovered over the pitch

25 Brian Little

26 Sheffield Wednesday 0 Villa 4

27 Sunderland

28 A: 6

29 Ray Graydon

30 Mick Wright

Answers - 1975-76   Back in the Top Flight

1 It featured colour photographs
2 Leeds United
3 Leighton Phillips
4 Ted McDougall
5 Rodney Marsh
6 Keith Leonard
7 Royal Antwerp
8 Ken Burns
9 Peter Withe
10 Dundee United
11 John Burridge
12 Villa 1 Royal Antwerp 5 (1-4 and 0-1)
13 Sheffield United
14 Coventry City
15 West Ham United
16 Southampton
17 Gordon Cowans
18 Chris Nicholl
19 None!
20 Manchester United and Liverpool

Answers - 1976-77 Goals, Goals, Goals, Replays, Replays, Replays

1 Mervyn Day
2 Tony Hateley
3 Brian Little
4 Villa 2 Glasgow Rangers 0
5 Alex Cropley
6 David O'Leary
7 Centre Back

180

8 Eintracht Frankfurt

9 Brian Little, John Deehan and Andy Gray

10 5-1

11 Highbury

12 Brian Little

13 The marching bandsmen believed a spur was left on the pitch after their half-time performance

14 Sheffield Wednesday

15 Manchester United

16 Chris Nicholl

17 Gordon Smith

18 Terry Darracott

19 True

20 Leighton Phillips

21 Joe Gallagher

22 Villa 4 West Bromwich Albion 0

23 Fourth

24 Southampton

25 Full Back

Answers - 1977-78 Return to European Action

1 John Gregory

2 Dennis Tueart

3 The New *North Stand* was opened to supporters

4 Fenerbache

5 Sir Alf Ramsay

6 Saudi Arabia

7 Gornik Zabrze

8 Liverpool 1 Villa 2

9 Tony Butler

10 Theme From an Unmade Silent Movie

11 Newcastle United

12 Johan Cruyff

13 Right Back

14 Ken McNaught and John Deehan

15 John Gidman

16 Barcelona 4 Villa 3

17 Tony Woodcock

18 Newcastle United

19 C: 6-1

20 Jimmy Rimmer

Answers - 1978-79 Million Pound Footballers

1 Hajduk Split

2 Gary Shelton

3 They beat a Tottenham Hotspur team 4-1 that included new signings Osvaldo Ardilles and Ricky Villa after their World Cup winning exploits for Argentina

4 Gary Shaw

5 Willie Young

6 Highfield Road, Coventry

7 Five

8 Remarkably, D: The Motor Show was on at the NEC.

9 They climbed up the floodlight pylon at the corner of Witton Lane and the Holte End

10 He had already played his last match before leaving Villa in the Summer

11 Allan Evans

12 John Deehan

13 Gary Shelton

14 Danny Blanchflower

15 Arnold Muhren

Answers - 1979-80 Comings and Goings

1 Burnley
2 Terry Donovan
3 Colchester United
4 Manchester United
5 Des Bremner
6 Mike Pejic
7 Mr Harry Kartz
8 West Bromwich Albion
9 A dog ran on the pitch
10 Eric Houghton
11 Les Sealey, Steve Hunt and Andy Blair
12 Nigel Spink
13 Gary Shaw
14 Terry Venables
15 Ray Stewart
16 Ken Swain
17 Robert Hopkins
18 Noel Blake
19 26
20 Manchester City

Answers - 1980-81 'Do You Want to Bet Against Us?'

1 Cambridge United
2 Leeds United
3 Maine Road
4 Ipswich Town
5 Emlyn Hughes
6 Villa 4 Sunderland 0
7 3-3 draws

183

8 Alex Sabella

9 They were the only "Brummies"

10 David Geddis

11 Stoke City

12 Tom/Thomas

13 Dennis Mortimer

14 (Ray and Alan) Kennedy

15 A new electronic scoreboard

16 Tony Morley

17 Gordon Cowans

18 Leicester City

19 Brendan Batson

20 Manchester City

21 Ken McNaught

22 Des Bremner

23 Gary Shaw

24 Peter Withe

25 Manchester City

26 Pele

27 Willie Young and Brian McDermott

28 Bosko Jankovic

29 None

30 The Rugby League Challenge Cup Final

Answers - 1981-82 Champions of Europe

1 East Germany

2 Villa 2 Spurs 2

3 Notts County

4 Tottenham Hotspur

5 Liverpool

6 Iceland

7 Nowhere! (or East Germany). Dynamo Berlin were in a pre-qualifying round with St Etienne, a fact that was stated in the article. Vainqueur Tour was the placeholder name for the winner of that tie, literally meaning 'round winner'. With the huge amount of information we have today, by comparison, the oversight was understandable.

8 Andy Gray

9 Boxes of Matches

10 Tony Morley

11 Gordon Cowans

12 Villa 0 Dynamo Berlin 1

13 Des Bremner

14 David Geddis, Notts County

15 West Bromwich Albion

16 A 1-4 defeat to Manchester United at Old Trafford

17 Peter Withe

18 Simferopol

19 Oleg Blokhin

20 A 0-0 draw

21 Ken McNaught

22 Le Coq Sportif

23 RSC Anderlecht

24 Tony Morley

25 Southampton and Brighton and Hove Albion

26 All of them!

27 Leeds United

28 Cyrille Regis

29 Swansea City

30 Feyenoord

31 B: Spink wore white shorts while Rimmer wore black

32 16

33 Brian Moore

34 D: Gary Shaw

35 Dieter Hoeness

36 Brian Clough

37 Tony Barton

38 Allan Evans and Ken Swain

39 Six

40 Sheffield

Answers - 1982-83 World Cup, World Club Cup, Super Cup

1 Kuwait

2 Allan Evans and Peter Withe

3 Erica Roe

4 Besiktas

5 It was ordered to be played behind closed doors, leaving less than 300 in the ground

6 Nottingham Forest

7 Gary Shaw

8 Mark Walters

9 The badge was moved from centre, the kit manufacturer's logo was on the chest instead of the sleeve and no sponsor's name was allowed

10 Uruguay

11 Villa 0 Penarol 2

12 Doug Ellis

13 Barcelona

14 Gary Shaw

15 Mark Walters

16 Gordon Cowans

17 Ken McNaught

18 Nine

19 Allan Evans (Which made him unavailable for the Juventus tie)

20 Paul Birch

21 Dino Zoff, Claudio Gentile, Antonio Cabrini, Gaetano Scirea, Marco Tardelli and Paolo Rossi

22 Michel Platini (France) and Zbigniew Boniek (Poland)

23 Gordon Cowans

24 Peter Withe

25 Sixth (only 3 points behind 2nd placed Watford)

Answers – Starting XI – Quiz 4

Carson

Bouma Mellberg Laursen Knight

Barry Petrov Reo-Coker Young

Carew Agbonlahor

Answers – Tenable – Quiz 4

1. Manchester United
2. Watford
3. West Ham United
4. Middlesbrough
5. Arsenal
6. Southampton
7. Chelsea
8. Fulham
9. Liverpool
10. Wycombe Wanderers

Answers – Map Quiz 2 – European Villans

Player	No	Player	No	Player	No
Fernando Nelson	3	Kosta Nedeljkovic	17	Andy Townsend	2
Andreas Weimann	15	Charles N'Zogbia	5	Aleksander Tonev	18
Benito Carbone	14	George Boateng	7	Jores Okore	9
Libor Kozak	20	Bjorn Engels	6	John Carew	12
Joey Gudjonnsen	1	Thomas Hitzlsperger	8	Filip Marschall	21
Gabor Kiraly	22	Robin Olsen	10	Alpay Ozalan	19
Phillipe Senderos	13	Carlos Cuellar	4	Peter Enkelman	11
Bosko Balaban	16				

Answers – Villanagrams 3

1 Mark Draper

2 Leon Bailey

3 Peter Crouch

4 Callum O'Hare

5 Stuart Gray

6 Libor Kozak

7 Paul Rideout

8 James Chester

9 Roberto Di Matteo

10 Simon Stainrod

11 Harry Parkes

12 Thomas Sorensen

13 Steven Gerrard

14 Jordan Ayew

15 Sam Hardy

16 Keinan Davis,,

17 Emile Heskey

18 Derek Mountfield

19 Steve Froggatt

20 Dean Smith

Answers – Starting XI – Quiz 5

Spink

Barrett Ehiogu McGrath Staunton

King Townsend Richardson Houghton

Saunders Atkinson

Answers – Tenable – Quiz 5

1 Cazoo
2 Intuit Quickbooks
3 Fx Pro
4 Acorns
5 DWS Investments
6 Rover
7 NTL
8 LDV Vans
9 AST Computers
10 Muller

Answers – Question Set Five – The Fall and Rise and the End of the Old Divisions

Answers - 1983/84 Away Day Blues

1 Napoli
2 Swindon Town
3 Steve McMahon
4 Romeo Zondervan and Martin Jol
5 Ken McNaught
6 Mark Walters
7 Barnsley
8 Vitória Guimarães
9 Colin Gibson
10 Noel Blake
11 Tony Woodcock
12 Spartak Moscow
13 Peter Withe
14 Norwich City
15 Everton
16 The first ever live televised league match from Villa Park
17 Peter Withe
18 Mark Jones
19 A: Derby County
20 All six!

Answers - 1984/85 Turning to Turner

1 Bayern Munich and Boca Juniors
2 Shrewsbury Town
3 He was the youngest ever Villa manager

4 Nottingham Forest

5 Didier Six

6 Gary Lineker

7 John Gregory

8 Southampton

9 Newcastle United

10 Tony Daley

11 Dennis Mortimer

12 Peter Withe

Answers - 1985/86 Low Gates

1 David Seaman

2 Simon Stainrod

3 Villa 8 Exeter City 1

4 Nobby Stiles

5 Paul Kerr and Steve Hunt

6 Portsmouth

7 Arsenal

8 Southampton

9 Oxford United and Paul Birch

10 Des Bremner

11 Watford

12 Birmingham (29 points), West Bromwich Albion (24 points)

Answers - 1986/87 The Dreaded Drop

1 Sheffield Wednesday

2 Tottenham Hotspur

3 John Fashanu and Kevin Gage

4 Ron Wylie

5 Liverpool

191

6 Allan Evans

7 Coventry City and West Ham United

8 Steve Hodge

9 Phil Robinson

10 Frank Upton

11 Manchester City and Leicester City

12 Tony Dorigo

Answers - 1987/88 Second Division – The 'Shambles'

1 Birmingham City

2 Warren Aspinall

3 Mark Lillis

4 Millwall

5 C: 6,000 goals

6 Stuart Gray and Andy Gray

7 Garry Thompson

8 Hull City

9 Gary Shaw

10 John Barnes and Peter Beardsley

11 Swindon Town

12 They scored 5 more goals, identical goal difference, same number of points!

Answers - 1988/89 A Season of Survival

1 Gordon Cowans

2 The Simod Cup

3 Bradford City

4 Lee Butler

5 Norwich City

6 Crewe Alexandra

7 David Platt
8 Newcastle United
9 Coventry City
10 One, they finished 17th

Answers - 1989/90 Graham Taylor's England CV

1 Alan McInally
2 Paul McGrath
3 Alvechurch
4 Sheffield Wednesday (Dalian and Ron Atkinson)
5 Stuart Gray
6 Everton
7 3-0
8 Selhurst Park
9 Middlesbrough
10 Oldham Athletic
11 Chris Price
12 Liverpool

Answers - 1990/91 Scored for Villa, Never played for Villa

1 Jozef Vengloš
2 Ivo Stas
3 QPR
4 Kent Nielsen
5 Jurgen Klinsmann
6 David Elleray
7 Steve Bruce
8 Derby County, Watford, Huddersfield Town
9 Gary Penrice
10 David Platt

11 Dwight Yorke
12 Sheffield United

Answers - 1991/92 Big Ron

1 Steve Staunton
2 Trevor Francis
3 Bournemouth
4 Ugo Ehiogu
5 Dariusz Kubicki
6 Stephen Froggatt
7 Stefan Beinlich
8 Liverpool
9 Tottenham Hotspur
10 Mark Bosnich
11 Cyrille Regis
12 B:16

Answers – Question Set Six – The Premier League Era

Answers - 1992-93 - The Premier League Begins

1 Ipswich Town
2 A:17,894
3 Sheffield United
4 Frank McAvennie
5 Ronnie Rosenthal
6 Dean Saunders, Ray Houghton and Shaun Teale
7 Coventry City
8 Gary Parker
9 Ipswich Town
10 Steve Staunton
11 Jonathan Gould
12 Blackburn Rovers, Oldham Athletic and QPR

Answers - Season 1993-94 Farewell Old Holte End

1 Andy Townsend
2 Portsmouth
3 Slovakia
4 Birmingham City
5 Mark Bosnich
6 Tony Daley
7 Alan Ball
8 D: Arsenal and Tottenham Hotspur
9 Dalian Atkinson
10 Saunders, Teale, Fenton, Atkinson, Daley
11 Andrei Kanchelskis
12 Liverpool

195

Answers - Season 1994-95 – That Muller Away Sponsored Shirt

1 John Fashanu
2 Gareth Southgate
3 Dennis Bergkamp
4 Nii Lamptey
5 Ray Houghton
6 Garry Parker, Steve Staunton, Andy Townsend and of course…..Phil King!
7 Michael Oakes
8 Trabzonspor
9 Wimbledon
10 Tottenham Hotspur
11 Leicester City
12 Ian Taylor
13 Glenn Hoddle
14 Tommy Johnson
15 A 4-4 draw
16 Coventry City
17 Four
18 Dwight Yorke
19 Paul McGrath
20 Norwich City

Answers - Season 1995-96 Great Cup Runs

1 Alan Hansen
2 Peterborough United
3 Carl Tiler
4 David Platt
5 Lee Hendrie
6 Gravesend and Northfleet
7 Gordon Cowans

8 Arsenal
9 A: 8
10 Savo Milosevic
11 Old Trafford
12 4th

Answers - Season 1996-97 Consistently Consistent

1 Sasa Ćurčić
2 West Bromwich Albion
3 Helsingborgs
4 Paul McGrath
5 Dwight Yorke
6 Wimbledon
7 Sam Allardyce
8 David James, Stan Collymore and Patrick Berger
9 Fabrizio Ravanelli
10 5th

Answers - Season 1997-98 UEFA Cup Run

1 Alan Wright
2 Chris Sutton
3 Bordeaux
4 Ian Taylor
5 Stan Collymore
6 Tim Sherwood
7 Coventry City
8 Brad Friedel
9 Barnsley
10 Athletico Madrid
11 Gareth Barry

12 Bolton Wanderers

Answers - Season 1998-99 A Season of Two Halves

1 David Unsworth
2 Alan Thompson
3 Darius Vassell
4 Fabio Ferraresi
5 Gianluca Vialli
6 Celta Vigo
7 Dion Dublin
8 Southampton
9 Arsenal
10 Adam Rachel
11 George Boateng
12 Gareth Barry

Answers - Season 1999-2000 At Last, an FA Cup Final

1 Alan Shearer
2 Steve Staunton
3 Darlington
4 Dion Dublin
5 West Ham United
6 Benito Carbone
7 Leicester City
8 Everton
9 Arsenal
10 Bolton Wanderers
11 Mark Delaney
12 Stone, Hendrie, Barry and Dublin
13 Tottenham Hotspur

14 6th

15 Chelsea, Roberto Di Matteo

Answers - Season 2000-01 Gallic Flair

1 Alpay Özalan

2 Fourteen

3 The Hawthorns

4 Luc Nilis

5 Manchester City

6 Paul Merson

7 Lee Hendrie

8 Belgium

9 Moustapha Hadji

10 Juan Pablo Angel

11 Paul Merson

12 Julian Joachim

Answers - Season 2001-02 Graham Taylor Part 2

1 Stade Rennais, Rennes

2 Croatia

3 Steven Gerrard

4 It was scored by a goalkeeper (Peter Schmeichel).

5 Bolton Wanderers

6 Prince Charles

7 Dinamo Zagreb

8 John Deehan

9 Thomas Hitzlsperger

10 Peter Crouch

11 Benito Carbone and Ugo Ehiogu

12 Everton

Answers - Season 2002-03 A "Lousy" Season

1 Lille
2 Hibernian and Ecuador
3 Peter Enckelman
4 Olaf Mellberg
5 David Elleray
6 Thomas Hitzlsperger
7 Liverpool
8 Rob Edwards
9 Dwight Yorke
10 Middlesbrough
11 Loftus Road
12 Robbie Savage
13 Joey Guðjónsson
14 Marcus Allbäck
15 True (2 Cup, 1 League)

Answers - Season 2003-04 Looking Upward

1 David O'Leary
2 Leicester City
3 Stefan Postma
4 Chelsea
5 Paul Scholes
6 Bolton Wanderers
7 Gavin McCann
8 Peru
9 Luke Moore
10 Darius Vassell
11 Ronny Johnsen
12 Newcastle United

Answers - Season 2004-05 Narrowly Missing Out

1 Martin Laursen
2 Matthieu Berson
3 Liverpool
4 League One
5 Eric Djemba-Djemba
6 Emile Heskey
7 Gareth Barry
8 Steven Taylor
9 Kieron Dyer and Lee Bowyer
10 Graeme Souness
11 Jlloyd Samuel
12 Nolberto Solano

Answers - Season 2005-06 'We're Not Fickle'

1 Kevin Phillips
2 Patrik Berger
3 19
4 Wycombe Wanderers 3, Aston Villa 8
5 Doug Ellis
6 Burnley
7 Doncaster Rovers
8 Liam Ridgewell
9 Leeds United
10 Luke Moore
11 Micah Richards, 17
12 Darius Vassell
13 'We just don't like you'
14 Gary Cahill
15 Stuart Taylor

Answers - Season 2006-07 Sir Doug Sells!

1 Reading (2-1)
2 Glasgow Celtic
3 Scunthorpe United
4 Didier Agathe
5 Crystal Palace
6 Ron Saunders
7 Henrik Larsson
8 Bolton Wanderers
9 John Carew
10 Shaun Maloney
11 Sheffield United
12 Bright Future

Answers - Season 2007-08 Olof's Farewell

1 West Ham United
2 Marlon Harewood
3 Wrexham
4 Zat Knight
5 Younès Kaboul
6 Gabriel Agbonlahor
7 Portsmouth
8 Stamford Bridge
9 Dutch (Van der Sar), French (Evra, Saha), English (Brown, Ferdinand and Carrick), Serbian (Vidic), South Korean (Ji-Sung Park), Brazilian (Anderson), Welsh (Giggs) and Portuguese (Ronaldo)
10 It was Villa's third goal of the game
11 John Carew and Ashley Young
12 He bought them all a Villa shirt

Answers - Season 2008-09 England Call Ups

1 Iceland

2 Manchester City

3 James Milner

4 Bulgaria

5 Ajax

6 French

7 MSK Zilina

8 Steve Sidwell and Ashley Young

9 Hull City

10 Emile Heskey

11 CSKA Moscow

12 Stoke City

13 Brad Friedel

14 Frederico Macheda

15 Newcastle United

Answers - Season 2009-10 Wembley Double

1 Rapid Vienna

2 Wigan Athletic

3 Stephen Warnock, James Collins and Richard Dunne

4 Three

5 Gabriel Agbonlahor

6 James Milner

7 Villa 6 Blackburn 4

8 Phil Dowd

9 Howard Webb

10 Chelsea won 7-1

Answers - Season 2010-11 Out of the Blue?

1 West Ham United
2 Andreas Weimann
3 Stephen Ireland
4 Gerard Houllier
5 Ian Holloway
6 Ciaran Clark
7 Michael Bradley
8 Kyle Walker
9 Darren Bent
10 Jean II Makoun
11 Gabriel Agbonlahor
12 Stewart Downing

Answers - Season 2011-12 In From the Blues!

1 Barry Bannan and Alan Hutton
2 Hereford United
3 Jermaine Jenas
4 Chelsea
5 Robbie Keane
6 Andreas Weimann
7 Australian
8 B, survival being down to the fact they drew so many games, which in turn also meant they had a healthier goal difference than those around them
9 Glasgow Rangers
10 West Ham United

Answers - Season 2012-13 The Wheels Start to Come Off

1 West Ham United and Everton
2 Enda Stevens
3 4-2
4 Jordan Bowery
5 Robert Snodgrass
6 Christian Benteke
7 Chelsea 8 Villa 0
8 Bradford City
9 Matt Lowton
10 Ron Vlaar
11 Brett Holman
12 Wigan Athletic

Answers - Season 2013-14 Lamentable Lambert, Consistently Poor, Inconsistently 'Excellent'

1 Antonio Luna
2 Nicklas Helenius
3 Karim El Ahmadi
4 Leandro Bacuna
5 Crystal Palace
6 Harry Maguire
7 Villa 4 West Brom 3
8 Norwich City
9 James Chester, Ahmed Elmohamady and Curtis Davies
10 Nathan Baker

Answers - Season 2014-15 'Wembley, Wembley'

1 Roy Keane
2 Tom Cleverley
3 One
4 Blackpool
5 Carles Gil
6 Bournemouth
7 Hull City
8 Scott Sinclair
9 Jack Grealish
10 QPR
11 Fabian Delph
12 Phillipe Coutinho
13 Sadio Mané
14 Danny Ings
15 John Moss

Answers - Season 2015-16 Unforgivably Catastrophic

1 Rudy Gestede
2 Micah Richards
3 Villa 5 Notts County 3
4 Jack Grealish
5 José Ángel Crespo
6 Manchester City
7 Wycombe Wanderers
8 Norwich City and Crystal Palace
9 Swansea City
10 Hope

Answers - Season 2016-17 Stopping the Rot

1 Pierluigi Gollini
2 Sheffield Wednesday
3 Rotherham United and Huddersfield Town
4 Tammy Abraham and Jonathan Kodjia
5 One
6 Burton Albion
7 Neil Taylor
8 Gabriel Agbonlahor
9 QPR
10 25

Answers - Season 2017-18 Last Gasp Heartbreak

1 Conor Hourihane
2 Keinan Davis
3 Barnsley
4 Jota
5 Bristol City
6 Peterborough United
7 Robert Snodgrass
8 Lewis Grabban
9 Villa 4 Wolves 1
10 Bolton Wanderers
11 Jack Grealish
12 4th
13 Tony Pulis
14 Mile Jedinak
15 Denis Odoi

Answers - Season 2018-19 'Allez Allez Allez'

1 Tottenham Hotspur
2 Tony Xia
3 Jonathan Kodjia and James Chester
4 Sheffield United
5 Barry Bannan
6 Yannick Bolasie and Glenn Whelan
7 Swansea City
8 Alan Hutton
9 5-4
10 Tammy Abraham
11 Jay Rodriguez
12 Steve McLaren
13 Tyrone Mings
14 Andre Green
15 Derby County
16 Jack Grealish
17 Rotherham United
18 Millwall
19 Mateusz Klich
20 Tyler Roberts
21 Patrick Bamford
22 Albert Adomah
23 Norwich City and Ipswich Town
24 Hourihane, Jedinak, Grealish and Abraham
25 Anwar El Ghazi

Answers - Season 2019-20 VAR

1 Wesley
2 Crewe Alexandra
3 Crystal Palace
4 Calum Chambers
5 5-1
6 Liverpool
7 Trézéguet
8 1-2
9 Leicester City
10 June
11 The players of both sides and officials took a knee
12 Orjan Nyland
13 Michael Oliver
14 Arsenal
15 Jack Grealish

Answers - Season 2020-21 The Strangest of Seasons

1 Sheffield United
2 Watkins (3), Grealish (2), Barkley and McGinn
3 John McGinn
4 Mike Dean
5 Crystal Palace
6 16
7 1-1
8 Jonathan Moss
9 Ollie Watkins
10 Phil Jagielka
11 Carney Chukwuemeka and Jaden Philogene-Bidace

12 Chelsea

Answers - Season 2021-22 Dean and Jack Leave

1 Cameron Archer

2 Kortney Hause

3 Wolverhampton Wanderers

4 Southampton (A)

5 Ezri Konsa

6 Michael Oliver

7 Duncan Ferguson

8 It was delayed until 15:30, The AMEX Stadium, Tim Iroegbuenam

9 Jesse Marsch

10 Dejan Kulusevski

11 Aston Villa 2-0 Norwich City

12 Burnley

Answers - Season 2022-23 Unai Emery's Claret and Blue Army

1 Diego Carlos and Boubacar Kamara

2 Aston Villa 2-1 Everton

3 It was scored direct from a corner by Douglas Luiz

4 Phillipe Coutinho

5 A 3-0 away defeat to Fulham

6 Aaron Danks

7 A 3-1 home win over Manchester United

8 Brighton and Hove Albion

9 Eight

10 Leicester City and Arsenal

11 AFC Bournemouth and Newcastle United

12 Jacob Ramsey

Answers - Season 2023-24 Champions League Qualification

1 Moussa Diaby
2 Italy (Udinese)
3 Villa 8-0 Hibernian
4 Group E
5 Clement Lenglet
6 Youri Tielemans
7 Cameron Archer
8 Matty Cash
9 McGinn, Watkins, Bailey, Tielemans, Moreno
10 Goodison Park
11 Jordan Henderson
12 Chris Kavanagh
13 Youri Tielemans
14 Tielemans, Watkins, Cash, Luiz
15 Ayoub El Kaabi
16 Italian
17 Callum Chambers
18 68
19 Ollie Watkins
20 Jhon Duran v Crystal Palace (H)

Answers – Starting XI – Quiz 6

Dunn

Bradley Turnbull Tiler Aitken

Hamilton Godfrey McMahon Anderson

Gibson Lochhead

Answers – Tenable – Quiz 6

1. Workington Town
2. Blackpool
3. Aston Villa
4. Crystal Palace
5. Queens Park Rangers
6. Wolverhampton Wanderers
7. Sheffield United
8. Southampton
9. Newcastle United
10. Hibernian

Answers – Who Am I?

1 Tammy Abraham

2 Derek Dougan

3 Con Martin

4 John Burridge

5 Emile Heskey

6 Mark Bosnich

7 Tony Cascarino

8 Stan Collymore

9 John Carew

10 James Chester

11 Eamonn Deacey

12 Peter Crouch

13 Earl Barrett

14 David Ginola

15 Ugo Ehiogu

16 Jonathan Kodjia

17 Ray Houghton

18 Derek Mountfield

19 Shaun Maloney

20 John Terry

Answers – Map Quiz 3 – England Villans

1. Chris Nicholl (Stockport, (Wilmslow))
2. Tony Hateley (Derby)
3. Darius Vassell (Birmingham)
4. Ashley Young (Stevenage)
5. David James (Aylesbury, (Welwyn))
6. Ugo Ehiogu (London, (Hackney))
7. Andy Townsend (Maidstone)
8. Gareth Barry (Tonbridge Wells, (Hastings))
9. Bruce Rioch (Guildford)
10. Martin Keown (Oxford)
11. Tyrone Mings (Bath)
12. Ray Graydon (Bristol)
13. Chris Price (Hereford)
14. John Sleeuwenhoek (Wolverhampton)
15. Frank Carrodus (Warrington, (Altrincham))
16. John Gidman (Liverpool)

Answers – 5 Aside: Former Favourites

Answers: 5 Aside: Stiliyan Petrov

1 Bulgaria
2 Glasgow Celtic
3 2008/09
4 19
5 Martin Laursen

Answers: 5 Aside: Alan Hutton

1 Alex McLeish
2 The Scottish Cafu
3 Paul Lambert
4 21
5 D:50

Answers: 5 Aside: Gabriel Agbonlahor

1 Erdington
2 Sheffield Wednesday
3 Everton
4 5
5 Germany, Spain and Belarus

Answers: 5 Aside: Charlie Aitken

1 660
2 Uncatchable
3 They were all headers
4 5
5 New York Cosmos

Answers - 5 Aside: Jhon Durán

1 Chicago Fire
2 Colombia
3 A: Header
4 Crystal Palace
5 Leicester City

Answers: 5 Aside: Juan Pablo Ángel

1 Martin O'Neill
2 Colombia
3 C: Fulham
4 River Plate
5 Portsmouth

Answers: 5 Aside: Alan McInally

1 Glasgow Celtic
2 Rambo
3 Costa Rica
4 Kilmarnock
5 Spurs

Answers: 5 Aside: Albert Adomah

1 Roberto Di Matteo
2 True
3 37
4 Ghana
5 Nottingham Forest

Answers: 5 Aside: Allan Evans

1 C: 472
2 True, Gary Shaw was second to last
3 1983/84
4 Liverpool
5 Dunfermline Athletic

Answers: 5 Aside: Ashley Young

1 17
2 Inter Milan
3 C: 2018
4 2008/09
5 Sir Lewis Hamilton

Answers: 5 Aside: Brian Little

1 1976/77
2 A: Fulham
3 Jersey
4 Wrexham
5 Royal Antwerp

Answers: 5 Aside: Christian Benteke

1 D:49
2 DC United
3 The FA Cup Final v Arsenal
4 3
5 20

Answers: 5 Aside: Dalian Atkinson

1 Fenerbahçe
2 They were all 1-1 draws
3 Sheffield Wednesday
4 Ipswich Town
5 Hans Segers

Answers: 5 Aside: Darius Vassell

1 John Gregory
2 2002 Japan/S.Korea
3 True
4 Leicester City
5 The Netherlands

Answers: 5 Aside: David Platt

1 Crewe Alexandra
2 Bradford City
3 Bari
4 England v Belgium
5 San Marino

Answers: 5 Aside: Dion Dublin

1 Leicester City
2 Cambridge United
3 Norwich City
4 Shay Given
5 Millwall

Answers: 5 Aside: Dwight Yorke

1 Trinidad and Tobago
2 5
3 Sunderland
4 Sydney FC
5 Villa (98 in all matches, league and cups)

Answers: 5 Aside: Tony Daley

1 17
2 Wolverhampton Wanderers, Watford and Walsall
3 Euro 1992
4 Ron Atkinson
5 Sheffield United

Answers: 5 Aside: Nathan Delfouneso

1 The Fonz
2 Burnley, Coventry or Leicester City
3 17
4 Blackpool
5 Chorley F.C.

Answers: 5 Aside: Mark Draper

1 8
2 Notts County
3 Manchester United
4 Southampton
5 Glenn Hoddle

Answers: 5 Aside: Jack Grealish

1 Notts County
2 41, 40 and 10
3 Dean Smith
4 Denmark
5 A: None, they lost every one

Answers: 5 Aside: Lee Hendrie

1 C: 250+
2 Czech Republic
3 15, 17, 7
4 Coventry City
5 Tamworth

Answers: 5 Aside: Conor Hourihane

1 Barnsley
2 West Bromwich Albion
3 Republic of Ireland
4 Swansea City
5 Bristol City

Answers: 5 Aside: Julian Joachim

1 Brian Little
2 Celta Vigo
3 Boston United and Darlington
4 D: 16
5 12

Answers: 5 Aside: Martin Laursen

1 AC Milan
2 England
3 Newcastle United
4 Juventus
5 Tottenham Hotspur

Answers: 5 Aside: Paul McGrath

1 C: 300+ (324)
2 True
3 Graham Taylor
4 1992/93
5 Derby County

Answers: 5 Aside: James Milner

1 11
2 C: 10
3 Moldova
4 Sunderland
5 Swindon Town

Answers: 5 Aside: Savo Milošević

1 A bandana
2 Coventry City
3 Real Zaragoza
4 5
5 Bosnia and Herzegovina

Answers: 5 Aside: Kevin Richardson

1 Real Sociedad
2 A: Newcastle-on-Tyne
3 B: Greece
4 Ron Atkinson!
5 Everton and Arsenal

Answers: 5 Aside: Dean Saunders

1 Swansea City and on loan to Cardiff City
2 Swindon Town
3 A: Ipswich Town
4 Sheffield United
5 C: Galatasaray

Answers: 5 Aside: Gareth Southgate

1 True
2 C: Leeds United
3 Crystal Palace and Middlesbrough
4 Leicester City
5 Pizza Hut

Answers: 5 Aside: Nigel Spink

1 D:17
2 Australia
3 Wigan Athletic and Sunderland
4 Millwall
5 Phil Neal and Ian Rush

Answers: 5 Aside: Ian Taylor

1 West Ham United
2 Graham Taylor
3 Wimbledon
4 Tayls Talking
5 John Rudge

Answers: 5 Aside: Gareth Barry

1 Chelsea
2 B: 440
3 Kevin Keegan
4 Spurs
5 15 and 24

Answers: 5 Aside: Paul Merson

1 False, he came from Middlesbrough
2 France 1998
3 He scored from the rebound of his own missed penalty kick, the second penalty miss by Villa in the match
4 Walsall
5 Portsmouth

Answers: 5 Aside: Ian 'Chico' Hamilton

1 Chelsea
2 Southend United
3 True
4 Minnesota Kicks
5 South Yorkshire (including Sheffield United and Rotherham United)

Answers: 5 Aside: Ron Saunders

1 Four
2 False, he was a centre forward
3 110%
4 Keith Coombes
5 Manchester United (Dec 2006, Guest of Honour) and Sheffield United (May 2007, 25th Anniversary of European Cup win)

Answers: 5 Aside: Ian Ross

1 Bill Shankley
2 Bruce Rioch
3 Sheffield Wednesday
4 FC Valur
5 Northampton Town

Answers: 5 Aside: James 'Jimmy' Cumbes

1 Tranmere Rovers
2 Don Howe
3 True (1hr on Sundays)
4 They all played first class cricket as well as football
5 Portland Timbers

Answers - 5 Aside: Douglas Luiz

1 Girona
2 Arsenal
3 Aleksandar Mitrovic
4 Juventus
5 Argentina

Answers – And Finally: Villa in Print

1 From Mine to Milan - Gerry Hitchens
2 Back from the Brink - Paul McGrath
3 Here, There and Everywhere - Shaun Teale
4 The Manager - Ron Atkinson
5 On Days Like These - Martin O'Neill
6 All for the Love of the Game - Peter Withe
7 One - Peter Schmeicel
8 Ask a Footballer - James Milner
9 In His Own Words - Graham Taylor
10 Hooked - Paul Merson
11 Deadly! - Sir Doug Ellis
12 The Road to Persia - Darius Vassell
13 Going for Goal - Peter McParland
14 Hail Cesar - Billy McNeill
15 The Curse of Pele -Nii Lamptey
16 Born to Score - Dwight Yorke
17 The Odd Man Out - Ron Saunders
18 Football With a Smile - Joe Mercer
19 The Boss - John Gregory
20 Achieving the Goal - David Platt

About The Author

Michael Baker has been supporting Villa since the late 1960's.
He has also been working with quizzes over 40 years, through writing
books, quiz question commissions, hosting and participating. A 25
year career in teaching also helped to sharpen his skills.

He has written several other quiz books:

On Football:

Ask Me Another: The Ultimate World Cup Quiz Book

*700 Questions on all things World Cup, published before the most
recent tournament in 2022*

From Rotherham to Rotterdam

*A journey in 500 questions through the Golden Era when Villa rose
from Division 3 to become Champions of Europe in just over a decade*

On Current Affairs:

The BIG QUIZ 2022

The BIG QUIZ 2023

The BIG QUIZ 2024

If You Enjoyed This Book

Please, would you mind leaving a review?
It really makes a massive difference to help self-published authors get noticed. It is really appreciated. Thank You

Recommendations

The primary sources in compiling this book are: My memory and my many copies of The Villa News and Record.

However, I have recently encountered a couple of sources which have impressed me greatly:

Aston Villa, The Complete Record by Rob Bishop and Frank Holt 2022 ISBN: 978-1-915571-27-4
In addition to the huge amount of information, I have yet to see another reference book of equivalent physical quality, which is just as well as I love reading it

www.avfchistory.co.uk   A continually developing website, full of information which is really well-maintained, well-presented and easily accessible

Printed in Dunstable, United Kingdom